Reading and Interpreting the Works of

EUGENE O'NEILL

Enslow Publishing
101 W. 23rd Street
Suite 240
New York, NY 10011
USA
enslow.com

Lit Crit
Guides

Reading and Interpreting the Works of

EUGENE O'NEILL

Spring Hermann

Published in 2017 by Enslow Publishing, LLC
101 W. 23rd Street, Suite 240, New York, NY 10011

Library of Congress Cataloging-in-Publication Data
Names: Hermann, Spring, author.
Title: Reading and interpreting the works of Eugene O'Neill / Spring Hermann.
Description: New York, NY : Enslow Publishing, 2017. | Series: Lit crit guides | Includes
  bibliographical references and index.
Identifiers: LCCN 2016004689 | ISBN 9780766079137 (library bound)
Subjects: LCSH: O'Neill, Eugene, 1888-1953--Criticism and interpretation--Juvenile literature. |
  O'Neill, Eugene, 1888-1953--Juvenile literature. | Dramatists, American--20th century--
  Biography--Juvenile literature.
Classification: LCC PS3529.N5 Z6757 2017 | DDC 812/.52 [B] --dc23
LC record available at https://lccn.loc.gov/2016004689

Printed in the United States of America

To Our Readers: We have done our best to make sure all website addresses in this book were active and appropriate when we went to press. However, the author and the publisher have no control over and assume no liability for the material available on those websites or on any websites they may link to. Any comments or suggestions can be sent by e-mail to customerservice@enslow.com.

Portions of this book originally appeared in *A Student's Guide to Eugene O'Neill*.

CONTENTS

Eugene O'Neill

Backstage Baby to Broadway Playwright

"I see life as a gorgeously-ironical, beautifully-indifferent, splendidly-suffering bit of chaos the tragedy of which gives Man a tremendous significance."

—Eugene O'Neill (1923)[1]

Eugene Gladstone O'Neill created the modern American drama, and for the first half of the twentieth century, he stood alone. He gave new meaning to the terms industrious and prolific, for in the thirty healthy years he enjoyed as a writer, he produced over fifty plays, many of them long, deeply complex works. Each of O'Neill's plays was original in approach, content, style, and structure. Many were beyond the ken of contemporary audiences and critics, yet as years passed and these plays were reexamined and revived, O'Neill's genius became more apparent. By the twenty-first century, almost every major American playwright credited his inspiration in some way to Eugene O'Neill. As playwright Tony Kushner put it: "He's the father of us all, the first to stake a claim nationally and internationally for American dramatic literature."[2]

O'Neill, like all artists, had to begin somewhere. Oddly enough, the first seven years of his life were lived backstage. Because his family used New York as a home base when his father, James O'Neill, was not touring as a theatre actor/manager, O'Neill's mother gave birth to him in 1888 in their hotel suite overlooking Times Square. At this time Eugene's elder brother James Jr. was in boarding school, so his mother packed the baby up and took him on the road with his father's company. Dressing rooms full of makeup and costumes, backstage wings, curtain calls, and roaring applause became the world of little Eugene. Highly intelligent and precocious, it was said Eugene memorized all his father's lines in his signature role as the count of Monte Cristo—and even knew his cues! In fact, it was Eugene that was waiting for his cue, although it would be many years in coming, to walk onto the Broadway stage and take his bow as an author.

The winter of 1920 found Eugene O'Neill pacing the streets of the New York theatre district near his birthplace. He knew his life's direction was about to take a radical change. He would no longer be known as the wastrel youngest son of the great actor James O'Neill. If his dream came true and his impending Broadway debut production succeeded, his years as a struggling, starving author could be over. His full-length drama *Beyond the Horizon* was about to open. Given to depression and a darker view of life, O'Neill could hardly believe his good fortune.

The winter of 1920, however, was a frightening time for Americans. An influenza epidemic spread across the nation. Due to alcohol addiction and a poor lifestyle, the tall, slender O'Neill was unhealthy and undernourished. It would be easy for him to contract the disease. Because his son Shane was an infant, O'Neill insisted that his wife, Agnes Boulton O'Neill, remain with the baby at their Provincetown, Massachusetts, house. He was afraid to expose them to illness in the city. The tension of final rewrites and a Broadway opening was made even worse because O'Neill missed his "Aggie" and their baby.

O'Neill was not unknown in New York. Already the author of twenty short plays, some had played from 1916 to 1919 in small New York theatres. "In the Zone," which opened in 1917, was reviewed quite positively by the critics, especially the prophetic Burns Mantle, who said: " . . . the one that leads is a sea tale told by Eugene O'Neill, son of James O'Neill the venerable and venerated actor, a new playwright who seems certain to be heard from again and most impressively heard from eventually."[3]

Yet O'Neill was hardly famous to Broadway audiences. So his producers opted for a series of matinees to showcase the new production. These performances would act as tryouts. If the show did well and a theatre opened up, *Beyond the Horizon* would run full-time on Broadway.

During the matinee of February 3, 1920, Eugene O'Neill hid behind the rear pillars of the Morosco Theatre. If the audience hated the play, he was in a good position to escape out the door. *Beyond the Horizon* was billed as an American tragedy. O'Neill feared the critics would not accept this work, at a time when no serious American tragedy had ever been produced. O'Neill glanced up to the boxes where James and Ella O'Neill sat ready to see their son's play open. After having gone through periods of angry separation from his seventy-four-year-old father, O'Neill now definitely wanted his approval. Brother James Jr., then forty-two, refused to attend. "Jamie" had wasted his talent as an actor as well as his father's support and was an unemployed alcoholic.

> **tragedy**
>
> A form of serious drama involving persons caught in calamitous circumstances.

The following day, with some reviews in hand, O'Neill wrote to his wife, Aggie, about his play: "It's positively stunning!

Whatever it may or may not do in a financial way, it has done all I ever expected of it already—and more."[4] James Sr., had wept with joy to see his son's playwriting on stage. *New York Times* critic Alexander Woollcott described the play in his review as "an absorbing, significant, and memorable tragedy, so full of meat that it makes most of the remaining fare seem like the merest meringue."[5] Ludwig Lewisohn of the *Nation* called it a full-bodied dramatic work, which established O'Neill on the same level as famed modern playwrights from Europe.[6]

Eugene O'Neill would explore many themes and concepts in his dramas throughout his productive career. He managed to touch on twelve of them in *Beyond the Horizon*:

1. **Modern drama in the form of a classic tragedy.** Some European playwrights were trying this form, which explores the individual's struggle with harsh fate and his relationship to God. Protagonists were taken from the common people. In *Beyond the Horizon*, O'Neill showed that humble Irish-American farmers deserved to have their personal struggle elevated to tragic drama.

2. **Self-absorbed protagonists.** These characters constantly examine their own self-image, trying to discover their inner dreams and needs. In *Beyond the Horizon*, the father and mother James and Kate Mayo, and their two sons, Andrew and Robert Mayo, explore their inner selves through a series of conflicts and discoveries.

3. **Denial of one's fated path.** In a tragedy, denial of one's fate in order to forge another path can bring sorrow and personal defeat. The bookish, poetic Robert Mayo says he prefers to go to sea but would stay to work the farm if needed. His brother Andrew replies: "Farming ain't your nature. There's all the difference shown in just the way us two feel

about the farm." Robert has to agree, telling Andrew: "You're wedded to the soil . . . Father is the same."[7] When Robert denies his destiny, takes Ruth (the girl his brother loves) as his wife, and attempts to farm, his tragic fate unfolds.

4. **Duty to one's family and land vs. desire for adventure abroad.** Deserting one's home was an issue for immigrants such as James O'Neill Sr. Born in 1846 in Thomastown, Ireland, James came to America at age six. His parents had been forced to relocate due to poverty and famine. Given his career as a traveling actor, the only home James could provide was the hotel nearest the next theatre, or a summer respite in their New London cottage. Andrew, the true farmer in the play, is driven off his land by losing Ruth. He swears: "I hate the farm . . . I'm sick of digging in the dirt and sweating in the sun like a slave without getting a word of thanks for it . . . If Uncle Dick won't take me on his ship, I'll find another."[8]

5. **Conflict of life on the land vs. life on the sea.** During O'Neill's youth, his boarding school and the family's summer cottage were located near the Connecticut shore. He made several voyages as a seaman, and lived as a young adult on Cape Cod. The seafaring life fascinated him. Similarly, protagonist Robert Mayo has romantic longings for the sailor's life. He tells his land-loving brother Andrew he wants "the beauty of the far off and unknown, the mystery and spell of the East which lures me . . . the freedom of the great wide spaces, the joy of wandering on and on—in quest of the secret which is hidden over there, beyond the horizon."[9]

6. **The emotional triangle between two men and a woman.** In *Beyond the Horizon*, the Mayo brothers both desire Ruth, the uneducated farm girl. Ruth feels a strong attraction to Robert, although she is loved deeply by Andrew. When Robert denies his fate to marry Ruth, forcing Andrew to leave

the farm he loves and go to sea, all three lives are set on an emotionally disastrous course. O'Neill had observed feelings of loss his mother expressed at leaving the genteel life for which she was intended in order to marry James O'Neill. The love triangle in *Beyond* sets the three protagonists on a course for tragedy. As her marriage and the farm both fail, Ruth screams at Robert: "You can go, and the sooner the better! I don't care! I'll be glad to get rid of you. The farm'll be better off too."[10] The eight years in the emotional lives of these three people reveal the damage they do to one another.

7. **The pain of unrequited love and the death of marital love.** For the Greek and Elizabethan authors of tragedy, this theme was a common one. Ruth declares that she has known for years it was Andrew she truly loved and desired, and when he returns they will be lovers. All Robert can do is shove Ruth away and insult her. The presence of their young child who binds Ruth and Robert together adds to the pain of their dying love. O'Neill himself had jumped into a brief early marriage in 1909 to Kathleen Jenkins to legitimize their baby, Eugene O'Neill Jr. Love died, and divorce followed. Although Kathleen and Eugene Jr. received alimony support from O'Neill and his father for many years, O'Neill knew he had distanced himself from his son. The sadness caused by such breakups for both adults and children became a common theme.

8. **Sibling rivalry vs. affection.** O'Neill's complex relations with his older brother Jamie obsessed him until Jamie's death, at the age of forty-five, from effects of alcoholism and a stroke. Jamie had influenced Eugene for his entire life. In *Beyond the Horizon*, the Mayo brothers' affection for each other, combined with streaks of jealousy and their inability to help each other recover their path, gives added depth to the tragedy.

9. **The need for a man to confront his father and please his mother.** In a theme that dates back to the Greek tragedy *Oedipus Rex*, O'Neill explores the pain that can result from a child's conflict with a parent. Robert Mayo, after deciding to remain home and marry Ruth, tells his father: "I'm going to settle right down and take a real interest in the farm, and do my share. I'll prove to you, Pa, that I'm as good a Mayo as you are—or Andy when I want to be."[11] The father knows this is false. Years pass and Robert fails in every way as a farmer, disappointing his parents deeply. As modern psychoanalysis became a part of O'Neill's life, he added techniques of regression and dreams to explore such characters' problems.

10. **Inherited weakness and illness.** This theme is touched on in *Beyond the Horizon*. Robert has survived tuberculosis (as did Eugene O'Neill), but the disease will return to claim his life. A weak constitution will also bring down Robert's young daughter Mary. In later works inherited weakness and deficiencies will play a larger role. Alcohol and drug dependencies, such as those in the life of his mother, Mary Ella O'Neill, and her father, Thomas Quinlan, figure in other O'Neill plays.

11. **The Irish tendency to believe in luck, curses, and destiny.** Being of Irish descent on both sides, O'Neill was steeped in his culture's superstitions, which seemed to contra-

O'NEILL'S "IRISHNESS"

Although O'Neill and his brother never visited their father's home, James Sr. stated that they had the map of Ireland on their faces.[12] A friend said about Eugene: "My God, when he looked at you he seemed to be lookin' right through you, right into your soul. He never said much and then spoke softly . . . He was a real Black Irishman."[13]

dict their major religion, Roman Catholicism. Ruth accuses Robert of bringing bad luck to the farm: "There's been a curse on it ever since you took hold. So go! Go and be a tramp like you've always wanted. It's all you're good for."[14] She believes in the Irish view of fate.

12. **The relative place of the poet-creator in modern society.** Like many artists before and after him, the young O'Neill had been a financial failure in the world. For many years his work as a playwright had not brought in enough money to support his children. He remained tied childishly at age thirty to the grudging support of his father. Protagonist Robert Mayo tries harder than O'Neill did to leave his books, fantasies, and writings behind and make a steady living. However, because he is denying his destiny, he brings down his farm and family. His spirit is not in tune with the farm. As the poet-creator, Robert might have found his true place and made a contribution to the world.

Beyond the Horizon, quickly recognized as the wave of the future in American drama, earned O'Neill his first Pulitzer Prize. Most American plays in the early twentieth century were still melodramatic. The protagonists may have faced difficulty and hardship, but in the end the lovers reunited and good always triumphed. O'Neill used a simple, realistic story line in *Beyond the Horizon*. His protagonists deny their fate, and their lives and luck grow worse. By the end, we must watch Robert die of consumption and exhaustion and join his deceased child. Ruth and Andrew find that life has beaten them down and they can no longer feel any passion for each other. The final speech by Andrew to Ruth as Robert dies is "Forgive me Ruth—for his sake—and I'll remember—I—you—we've both made a mess of things. We must try to help each other—and—in time—we'll come to know what's right—And perhaps we . . . "[15] Stage directions indicate Ruth must look as if she is beyond hope. Audiences reportedly sat in stunned silence at early performances when the curtain fell. Could this be the end for this family? Only after realizing they had seen a new kind of reality brought to the stage did they burst into applause.

In 1923, a reporter asked O'Neill why he wanted to write American tragedy. He said: "What I am after is to get an audience to leave the theatre with an exultant feeling from seeing somebody on stage facing life, fighting against the eternal odds. . . the individual life is made significant just by the struggle."[16]

O'Neill would write many kinds of tragedies for the stage over the course of his career, using realism, naturalism, expressionism, and symbolism as styles to get his meaning across to audiences. Concepts from past tragic authors inspired his creativity, combined with his imagination and life experiences.

This innovative mix of classical themes and personal traumatic conflicts require study of O'Neill's private life to truly appreciate his plays.

> **melodrama**
>
> A style of playwriting where good and evil were clearly portrayed, characters were mainly two-dimensional, and the resolution always rewarded the good and the just.

> **style**
>
> In theatre, a mode of expression and method of presentation.

"I've Knocked About a Bit": O'Neill's Rough Youth Reflected in Early Works

"It is difficult these days to realize that . . . a play of any imagination, originality or integrity by an American was automatically barred from a hearing in our theatre . . . the most vital thing for us . . . as possible future artists and creators to learn was to believe in our work. And to hope. He helped us to hope."

—Eugene O'Neill, crediting his 1914 Harvard drama professor George Pierce Baker with helping birth a new generation of playwrights[1]

To interpret Eugene O'Neill's complex themes and his approach to his characters, it is helpful to learn about his family and his unusual upbringing. Eugene's father, James O'Neill, immigrated to Buffalo, New York, in 1851. All of the O'Neills had to work as laborers, laundresses, or household help to survive. Even at age six, James understood the hard facts of life. After almost five years, James' father, Edward (his Americanized name) O'Neill, an alcoholic, supposedly wanted to die in his homeland. He stunned his family by deserting them and returning to Ireland. Edward Jr., (age eleven) and James (age ten) struggled to help the family by working in factories and machine shops. The boys saw many Irish women and children sent to the poorhouse, a miserable institution for paupers. James lived in dread his entire life of being sent there.

James O'Neill moved with his mother and siblings to Cincinnati, Ohio, where his older sister Josephine had married a tavern owner. A voracious reader, he was self-educated, and became an actor purely by chance. Strong, sturdy, with dark curly hair and very handsome features, he developed his powerful voice and became a popular young performer. By 1870, James O'Neill was playing leading roles at the Academy

O'Neill's father, James, was a stage and film actor. He appeared in the 1913 film version of *The Count of Monte Cristo*.

of Music, a theatre in Cleveland. There he co-starred with the best actors of his day.

In 1871, at age twenty-six, he met the shy daughter of a Cleveland merchant, fourteen-year-old Mary Ellen Quinlan. After she finished Catholic boarding school in Indiana, Mary Ellen began to call herself "Ella." A slender, pretty brunette, Ella liked music and studied the piano. She had suffered a terrible loss when her father died of alcoholism and tuberculosis in May 1874. Although she had no knowledge of the difficult life of a traveling actor, Ella believed she could be happy married to the dashing James O'Neill. For Ella, James kept the spirit of her father alive. For James, Ella would ward off his loneliness and place him securely in middle-class society.

Those who knew them well said that James and Ella deeply cared for each other for the forty-three years they were married. However, the divisions between them regarding money and power showed their sons that they were hardly the perfect couple. As a traveling actor's wife, Ella adapted to hotel living and never learned to cook. She reportedly made friends with several actresses and helped James learn his roles. Ella realized she might never have a permanent home due to James's career, so she stayed by his side, even when pregnant. James Jr. was born in 1878 while the company played in San Francisco. His parents called him Jamie.

In the summer of 1883, James bought a house in New London, Connecticut, a harbor town where the Thames River meets Long Island Sound. Ella's mother, Bridget Quinlan, already had a place there near her married sister. The O'Neills' rustic cottage on Pequot Avenue was the only home Ella and James ever shared.

When Eugene Gladstone O'Neill was born, Ella had already endured losing a child. Her second son, Edmund, contracted

This portrait of young Eugene was taken in the early 1890s.

measles at 18 months, probably from Jamie, while the boys were staying with Ella's mother. Before Ella made it back home from traveling with James, Edmund died. On March 4, 1885, having received a telegram about Edmund's death, James still played his evening performance. Filled with grief and guilt, Ella blamed James, her mother, Jamie, and herself for the baby's death.

On October 16, 1888, with ten-year-old Jamie in boarding school, Ella gave birth to another son, Eugene. Unfortunately this event brought more problems. Although James took time off from touring to be with Ella, the birth in the New York Barrett House, a residential hotel, was difficult. To ease her pain and postpartum depression, James suggested the hotel doctor prescribe morphine, the most common drug given women at this time. Ella struggled with morphine addiction for the next twenty-five years.

The effect of morphine ingested by baby Eugene through his mother's milk is hard to determine. Doctors today would say that the drug could have made Eugene nervous, irritable, and caused him to have a poor appetite. It might have damaged his entire nervous system. To help care for the fretful baby, James hired a nanny named Sarah Jane Sandy. Historian Stephen A. Black states that Sandy became "governess to Eugene and companion to Ella; she would be the boy's substitute mother until he was seven."[2] Sandy's help made it possible for Ella and Eugene to travel.

Eugene spent his childhood in hotels, on trains, and most importantly, in theatres. By the time Eugene was old enough to realize what his father was doing onstage, James O'Neill was starring in a production he owned and managed, *The Count of Monte Cristo*. As historian Louis Sheaffer put it, the boy "knew the entire play as well as he knew his Catechism; it was bred into his bones, . . . part of his blood stream, part of his breathing . . . Edmond Dantes [James O'Neill's role] was virtually a fifth member of the family."[3]

Critics have wondered how much Eugene was affected by the story of Edmond Dantes, a hero who was wronged by society and imprisoned, living mainly for revenge. Apparently O'Neill grew up with relationship problems, distrustful, suspicious of strangers, overly sensitive to criticism. His plays were his way of dealing with these issues. In the last interview he gave, O'Neill said: "Revenge is the subconscious motive for the individual's behavior with the rest of society."[4]

Eugene O'Neill spent his first seven years with adults, except for summers with a few children in New London. Ella O'Neill and the theatre company treated him like a pampered mascot. His difficulties with social adjustment and his juvenile approach to problems long after he came of age are understandable. He never had to mature like other boys. His dark imagination was honed by his nanny, Sarah Sandy, who liked to amuse him with tales of ghosts and murder. If they were staying in a city with a wax museum displaying violent characters, Sandy took Eugene for a scary visit.

During family summer vacations, Eugene developed a love of swimming in Long Island Sound and watching the ships come and go in New London harbor. A neighbor on Pequot Avenue, Margaret Kiley, said Eugene became "a fish, a regular water rat, forever playing around in the water."[5] His older brother, Jamie, did not care for swimming or sailing. As a troubled teenager, this young man learned to drink and visit the brothels of Bradley Street.

At age seven, Eugene was enrolled in a private boarding school in Riverdale, New York. The Academy of Mount St. Vincent was a strict Catholic school that had academies for both girls and boys. Jamie attended a nearby prep school in the Bronx. Sarah Sandy would stay in New York to meet the boys on holidays. Yet Eugene was frantic at being left at school. Later he said he hated his father for separating him from his mother. He could not accept that his father only wanted to give his sons a proper education, something he had been denied.

The first way Eugene O'Neill learned to get through his separation anxiety was by writing letters. As soon as he was old enough to spell, Eugene sent a deluge of letters to his parents at their theatre company, to his brother Jamie at school, and to nanny Sarah Sandy back in New York. For several years Eugene's roommate at the Academy was an orphan, Joseph McCarthy. Three years older than Eugene, McCarthy told historians Arthur and Barbara Gelb that Eugene came to value him as his only friend. They kept in touch through the 1930s, when Eugene wrote to McCarthy fondly about their school days. "Most boys liked him, too," said McCarthy, "though they considered him a little queer. He read Kipling and authors way beyond his years."[6] McCarthy remembered how much Eugene adored Jamie. By the time Jamie turned twenty, he was a student at St. John's College and had become a cynical alcoholic. His influence on Eugene was increasingly negative.

In the fall of 1900, when Eugene was twelve, Ella and James tried making a home in New York. Eugene went to day classes at De La Salle Institute on Fifty-ninth Street. Ella "kept house" in their residential hotel suite. Unfortunately, one day Eugene came home from class early and caught Ella giving herself a morphine injection. This was his first hint of why his mother was often so distant and moody.

When James Sr. and Jamie—who knew all too well of Ella's drug addiction—told Eugene that it stemmed from his difficult birth, Eugene blamed himself. At age thirteen, he prayed that if he would make excellent grades and do good works, God would cure Ella's addiction. Two years later, when she had not been "cured," fifteen-year-old Eugene turned his back on God and the Catholic Church and did not attend Mass again.

Eugene's next school was Betts Academy in Stamford, Connecticut. He got a solid formal education at Betts, but also took up the habits of smoking and drinking. Other Betts students recalled Eugene as being a popular fellow who liked breaking the rules and flouting the administration's authority. He was known by his pals as "Gene," the worldly son of a famous actor. In truth, Eugene was immature and romantic. In spite of Jamie dragging him to prostitutes, he respected the goodness of women.

The spring and summer of 1906 in New London were immortalized by O'Neill in his play *Ah, Wilderness!* O'Neill admitted later that the play was wish fulfillment: "The truth is, I had no youth."[7] For the first half of that summer, Eugene at age seventeen was parent-free, hanging out with Jamie. Ella and James Sr. were tourists in England and Ireland. Ella

Sanitariums for Drug Addicts

The use of opiates (referred to as laudanum) was common among Victorian women. Physicians readily prescribed them. An 1867 study showed that rural women considered opiates as the safest remedy for depression, preferable to alcohol. When a woman's drug addiction became severe, few sanitariums were available. In 1905–06 when Ella O'Neill detoxed from morphine, she might have been helped by St. Saviors Sanitarium or Brooklyn Home for Habitues, both in New York. Many women used mineral water spas such as the ones in Brattleboro and Saratoga for detoxification.

was "on the cure," meaning she had detoxed from morphine at a sanitarium. Eugene swam, sailed, and had dates with local girls. He also drank with Jamie at the local tavern and patronized the town's prostitutes. Having been accepted at Princeton University, Eugene assumed he was prepared to breeze through with his Betts education under his belt. He was tall and slim, with a handsome, chiseled face and thick brunette hair. Pampered by his parents, he wore tailored clothes and had the use of a car.

When Ella and James returned in August, the summer of 1906 grew more stifling in terms of weather and family emotions. This experience, plus the fog-bound summer of 1905, combined into one in O'Neill's memory. In the 1940s, he wrote a drama that used experiences from these two summers to expose the painful weaknesses of his family as they were locked together on a *Long Day's Journey Into Night*.

In the fall of 1906, O'Neill entered Princeton University. Although he was very well read, O'Neill did not fit in there. Freshman year was full of boyish rituals, including wearing black clothing and a beanie, plus chapel attendance and required introductory courses. Most freshmen embraced these experiences to be part of the group. O'Neill was a rebel from the start, to the fascination of his classmates. A dorm mate was stunned to see O'Neill's room décor: "He had a fish net up on the wall with souvenirs hanging from it, almost all of them theatrical: actresses' slippers, stockings, brassieres, playbills, pictures of chorus girls in tights . . . and several condoms."[8]

However, O'Neill had no better place to go than college. So he stayed at Princeton, drank at bars in nearby Trenton, New Jersey, and read voraciously. He used to quote aloud from his favorite poets, Swinburne and Lord Byron, especially a verse from Byron's *Childe Harold's Pilgrimage*: "I stood among them, but not of them; in a shroud of thoughts which were not their thoughts . . ."[9] O'Neill expressed his distance from his Princeton classmates with this quote.

On many weekends, O'Neill returned to his family's hotel suite in New York and prowled the bars in Greenwich Village and the Lower East Side. He also began seeing a married woman in Trenton, who would let him spend the night with her. He attended classes just often enough not to flunk out, but he seldom did the required work.

O'Neill did have an important theatre experience during his spring 1907 semester. In 1938, O'Neill was asked if he remembered the first time he encountered the work of the Norwegian playwright Henrik Ibsen. He replied: "I do remember well the impact upon me when I saw an Ibsen play

Growing up, O'Neill spent many summers in New London, Connecticut (seen here), where he developed a love for the sea.

for the first time, a production of *Hedda Gabler* at the old Bijou Theatre in New York—and then went again and again for ten successive nights. That experience discovered an entire new world of the drama for me. It gave me my first conception of a modern theatre where truth might live . . . Not long ago I read all of Ibsen's plays again. The same living truth is still there."[10] This 1907 production starred Alla Nazimova as Hedda. Coincidentally, another American playwright, Tennessee Williams, saw Nazimova star in Ibsen's *Ghosts* in 1934 and identified this Ibsen experience as the one that inspired him to begin playwriting.

After cutting too many classes and getting into a fight when returning drunk from Trenton, Princeton's administrators (former U.S. president Woodrow Wilson headed the university then) suspended Eugene O'Neill for "poor academic performance." At this point in his life, O'Neill had no goals. He breezed around New York, bummed money from his father, and began a love affair with a woman named Kathleen Jenkins. Both families disapproved of the affair because O'Neill was not able to support a wife.

In the fall of 1909, O'Neill was scheduled to sail to Central America, a plan James O'Neill Sr. set up to get his son away from Kathleen Jenkins. He was to go with Earl and Ann Stevens on a gold prospecting expedition in Honduras. Before he left, Eugene and Kathleen hurried to Hoboken, New Jersey, for a private wedding at Trinity Church. Kathleen was two months pregnant with Eugene's child. At age twenty-one, O'Neill would become a deadbeat husband and father.

O'Neill knew Kathleen and his baby would become one more responsibility for James Sr. When he looked back after his father died, O'Neill admitted that his father should have given up on him: "If anything, he was too patient with me.

What I wonder now is why he didn't kick me out. I gave him every chance to."[11]

In Honduras, Eugene encountered no gold—only malaria. He returned to New York to recuperate. O'Neill showed shocking indifference when Eugene O'Neill Jr. was born on May 4, 1910. From 1910 through 1912, Eugene sailed all over the world. He signed on for two voyages: to Buenos Aires, Argentina, in 1910, and to Southampton, England, in the fall of 1911. Although he worked hard as a sailor, he spent all his pay and was often penniless. He did, however, absorb a priceless amount of colorful material.

During a stay in Buenos Aires, O'Neill recalled going to a large sailors' café: "There the seamen yarned of adventures, boasted of his exploits to officially pretty ladies, drank, played cards, fought and wallowed."[12] After wallowing with them for a year, O'Neill sailed to South Africa and England, before returning to America. His love of seafaring stayed with him. Not that the sailor's life was glamorous—it was hard, rugged, honest, and often dangerous. Yet the language, the songs, the sounds and smells, and most of all the camaraderie lent a stark beauty to life working on a ship. O'Neill was always proud that he had been an able-bodied seaman.

During the winter of 1912, O'Neill lived in New York, existing on a dollar-a-day handout from his father. This allowed him to rent a cheap room over a saloon with a free lunch and just enough left over to get drunk each night. His alcoholism forced him into the life of a derelict. After his divorce from Kathleen was filed, he got a bottle of Veronal, an opiate alcoholics used to reduce the effects of hangovers. O'Neill took all the pills at once in a botched suicide attempt. Two of his fellow boarders found him and managed, though drunk themselves, to get him to Bellevue Hospital just in time. So O'Neill's life continued its dark path to nowhere.

From August to December 1912, Eugene did try to save himself. He signed on as a reporter for the New London *Telegraph*, earning $10 a week. He did a poor job of reporting, and the rumor was that his father was secretly paying his salary. During this period he fell in love with Maibelle Scott, an eighteen-year-old from a respectable New London family. Although O'Neill tried to be polite and sober in Maibelle's company, her father knew the twenty-four-year-old would-be writer was unsuitable. He forbade the match. The secret relationship between O'Neill and Maibelle became the inspiration for the love affair between Richard and Muriel in *Ah, Wilderness!*.

By December 1912, O'Neill contracted tuberculosis. His frightened parents sent him to Gaylord Farm, a private sanatorium in Wallingford, Connecticut, now known as Gaylord Hospital. He was an in-house patient until June 1913. Sober from the treatment regime at Gaylord, the playwright within Eugene O'Neill began to emerge. In 1923, O'Neill recalled: "At Gaylord my mind got the chance to establish itself, to digest and evaluate the impressions of many past years in which one experience had crowded on another . . . I thought about life for the first time, about past and future."[13]

For another sixteen months, O'Neill boarded with a New London family, where he swam, exercised, tried to stay off alcohol, and wrote short plays. These were rough works that did not attract a producer in New York, but O'Neill continued undaunted. By the spring of 1914, O'Neill had written *Bound East for Cardiff*, a one-act play based on his experiences as a seaman.

Surviving Tuberculosis

Few effective treatment facilities for tuberculosis (also called consumption) existed in 1912. Gaylord Farm Sanitarium in Wallingford, Connecticut, tackled the leading cause of death in America through keeping the patient rested, clean of substance abuse, well fed, and mentally strong. At age twenty-four, O'Neill was described by a Gaylord official as a patient who "came here on his hands and knees and left with a new sense of who he was."[14] Although many patients did relapse, O'Neill stayed free of the disease forever.

Another wonderful event in the family happened that spring. Perhaps overwhelmed with gratitude for Eugene's return to health, Ella O'Neill tried one more time to cure her addiction to morphine. This time she took the cure at the hands of compassionate nuns in a convent in New York, drawing on the roots of her childhood faith. And this time, it worked. To Eugene's joy, Ella stayed clear of morphine for the rest of her life.

That fall, O'Neill enrolled at Harvard University, specifically to take George Pierce Baker's dramatic composition course. James O'Neill Sr. hoped that studying at Harvard would help make Eugene a better professional writer, so he chipped in for the tuition. Most of Eugene's work from Baker's course has not survived, but his promise as a playwright was noted by his professor, and envied by his fellow students.

Although he did well in Baker's course, O'Neill again felt like a misfit. He retreated to a reclusive life in Greenwich Village, in a cheap room with another alcoholic friend, Terry Carlin. His renewed sobriety and health dissolved into an almost-fatal yearlong binge. Carlin kept O'Neill alive by forcing him to eat. To help O'Neill regain some strength, Carlin took him out to Provincetown on Cape Cod. There, some of Carlin's Greenwich Village buddies were putting together a small experimental theatre. Dragging O'Neill to one of their first meetings, Carlin made him present the troupe with his *Bound East for Cardiff*. As O'Neill read the script aloud, steeling himself for criticism, the Provincetown Players realized they had discovered an author capable of writing in an exciting, modern style. They welcomed him to the group.

Finally Eugene O'Neill was surrounded by artists who understood his potential as a playwright. He began to discover his true confidence, and his life changed forever.

FROM SMALL PLAYS A FULL-BLOWN HIT WILL GROW

"All the world will know Gene's plays some day . . . Gene's plays aren't the plays of Broadway; he's got to have the sort of stage we're going to found in New York."

—George Cram "Jig" Cook, 1916[1]

O'Neill fell in love with life in Provincetown—and became extremely fond of some of the players. Members such as journalist-writer John "Jack" Reed and producer-actor George Cram "Jig" Cook had enough money to rent houses on the Cape and put out some food. O'Neill lived off their support and became the principal author. Along with founder and playwright Susan Glaspell and a few others, the Provincetown Players gave experimental playwrights a place to grow and get produced. Their playhouse was a remodeled warehouse on a wharf. "The sea has been good to Eugene O'Neill," Susan Glaspell recalled. "It was there for his opening (of *Bound East for Cardiff*)."[2] The surf, the wind, the fog, and the fog bell, were provided by real life. The audiences loved the show.

Between productions put on in Provincetown and in a small theatre at 139 Macdougal Street in New York City, O'Neill worked with the Provincetown Playhouse from 1916 through 1925. This theatre formed the experimental laboratory for his development.

PROVINCETOWN, MASSACHUSETTS

The village at the tip of Cape Cod has existed for centuries as a center for fishing, and recently, for art and drama. The Provincetown Art Association and Museum was founded in 1914. In 1915 the Provincetown Players Theatre started in Joe and Mary O'Brien's fish-house at the end of their wharf. Because O'Neill's *Bound East for Cardiff* originated there, locals consider Provincetown the birthplace of modern American theater.

O'Neill's nautical short play, *Bound East for Cardiff*, was quite the hit on the wharf of Provincetown in 1916. Whether it would succeed with Greenwich Village audiences at the New York Playwrights' Theatre was the big question. O'Neill and the Provincetown company pitched in to make it work.

O'Neill took a room near the Washington Square apartment of John "Jack" Reed and Louise Bryant. Bryant, a writer and staple of the company, fell passionately for O'Neill. He spent most of his time at 193 Macdougal Street, the house that had been turned into the playhouse. Although he had no training in staging, O'Neill directed *Bound East for Cardiff*. He also worked on his one-act *Before Breakfast*, which premiered in December at the Playwrights' Theatre.

Only seven pages long, *Bound East for Cardiff* features eleven men who work on the tramp steamer *Glencairn*, bound for Cardiff, Wales. An intense character study of hardworking seamen of various nationalities, the play follows the slow, wrenching death of Yank from an accidental fall. How the crew and captain interact as they lose one of their own makes the brief drama powerful. O'Neill's years as an able seaman on tramp steamers around the world gave him plenty of detailed material, a kind of reality not seen on New York stages.

Before Breakfast, a complete change of setting and pace, was inspired by a play by August Strindberg. It gave the Playwrights' Theatre's leading actress a chance to shine. An eight-page solo performance by a downtrodden wife, Mrs. Rowland rails against her husband, Alfred, who is closeted in the bedroom. The audience is both enthralled and repelled by Mrs. Rowland, whose jobless husband writes poetry and drinks with the Greenwich Village art crowd while she makes a meager living sewing. We see only Alfred's hand as he reaches for a bowl of warm water to shave, described by O'Neill as "a sensitive hand with slender fingers."[3] Even in such a brief work, O'Neill still gives the audience a premonition of the final tragic moment, when Mrs. Rowland yells into Alfred's room: "What are you doing   still shaving, for heaven's sake? You'd better give it up. One of these mornings you'll give yourself a serious cut."[4] At the finale, Mrs. Rowland hears a groan and a crash, stares into the bedroom, then screams to see her husband has killed himself with the razor.

Audiences, and the one New York critic who reviewed it, liked *Bound East for Cardiff*. Even James O'Neill Sr., Eugene's toughest critic, was favorably impressed. Eugene went back to Cape Cod and used the off-season to write. His next three sea plays, *In the Zone* (produced in October 1917), *The Long Voyage Home* (produced in November 1917), and *Moon of the Caribbees* (produced in December 1918), drew once more on O'Neill's knowledge of the adventure and the hardship in a sailor's life.

O'Neill's approach was to write from a position of neutrality toward his characters. He did not make judgments or contrive to make characters behave in a certain way. No character was

O'Neill and the Provincetown Players were based here on the Lewis Wharf in Provincetown, Massachusetts.

forced to be a hero or a villain. O'Neill indicated in *Moon of the Caribbees* that the spirit of the sea was the hero. He maintained that a human being is not the center of the universe, or ever in complete control of his future. As Stephen Black puts it, "His tragic vision was neither pessimistic nor optimistic, but in it, the power of nature took precedence over the power of human beings."[5]

During this period he met his second wife, beautiful romance writer Agnes Boulton. Known to their friends as Gene and Aggie, the couple quickly fell in love and ran off to live together in Provincetown, where they married on April 12, 1918. James O'Neill Sr. approved of this marriage, thinking his son would be a stable working playwright with Agnes in charge of the house. O'Neill actually sold a play to a traveling troupe, which gave the couple an income. Productions from the Players Theatre brought money as well. It was obvious to all that O'Neill had no sense of responsibility regarding finances. Everyone hoped Agnes would change that pattern and keep them solvent.

The Rope was produced by the Provincetown Players in New York in April 1918, soon after Eugene O'Neill married. The cast of *The Rope* is centered on religious-fanatic farmer Abraham Bentley, his daughter Annie, his Irish son-in-law Pat Sweeney, and their child Mary, a ten-year-old girl described as having a "stupidly expressionless face" and hands that flutter aimlessly in "flabby gestures."[6] Grandfather Bentley yells at the child "you . . . brat! Spawn o'Satan, spyin' on me!"[7] Bigotry, familial hatred and greed, and hypocritical attitudes shape the story. The only light in little Mary's life shines when her sailor uncle, Luke, shows up. When Luke asks if his father is as stingy as ever, Pat Sweeney tells him: "if he owned the ocean, he wouldn't give a fish a drink."[8] The two conspire to find the old man's hidden fortune, but in an ironic twist, little Mary happens on the treasure herself. At curtain, Mary is happily using the gold coins as skipping stones into the sea! Echoes of the father and son relationships that inform *Desire Under the Elms* can be seen in *The Rope*.

The year 1919 proved to be full of blessings for O'Neill. His son Shane was born in October, and his *Moon of the Caribbees and Six Other Plays of the Sea* became his first published volume. In October 1919, another "kid" was born—and a totally new theme for O'Neill was explored in his short play *The Dreamy Kid*.

The Dreamy Kid explores a culture that O'Neill knew mainly by observation, that of urban African Americans. This would be the first of three plays O'Neill would write about black people, the only major white playwright to do so. Its production was one of the first by a white theatre company to employ a black cast. In this short work, four characters converge in a tiny Harlem apartment on what O'Neill called Carmine Street. Mammy Saunders is an elderly woman in her nineties, withered by old age and sickness. Beside her bed is her friend and caregiver, a middle-aged woman named Ceely Ann. A prostitute named Irene interrupts them, looking for The Dreamy Kid, Mammy's grandson. The Dreamy Kid, most likely in his twenties, finally arrives because he has been told his grandmother is dying. These four interact over two main issues: the dying of Mammy and the threat of police apprehension of The Dreamy Kid. O'Neill probably based the story on true tales about young African Americans involved with crime and gun violence in New York.

The Dreamy Kid covers a climactic point in the lives of this African-American family. O'Neill uses black dialect and raw emotion to carry the audience to the tragic conclusion.

O'Neill, his wife Agnes, and their son Shane, spend time on Cape Cod in 1922.

When the Dreamy Kid tells Ceely Ann he is wanted for shooting a white man, she moans, "May de good Lawd pardon yo' wickedness! Oh Lawd, what yo' po' old Mammy gwine say if she hear tell—and she never knowin' how bad you's got."[9] The dying of Mammy and the destruction of her grandson, whose wistful quality so moved her to give him the nickname, are inevitable but not actually shown onstage.

Like many of O'Neill's works, there is no solid conclusion or message to the play. Both Mammy and the Dreamy Kid call upon Jesus, each for their own needs. When Mammy hears singing in her head, she believes "hit's de singin' hymns o' de blessed angels I done heah fum above. Bless Gawd!"[10] As the curtain falls, the Dreamy Kid has stayed with Mammy until her death, which puts him into the hands of the police.

The Emperor Jones, begun in 1919, also explored African-American protagonists. This thirty-two-page work in eight scenes follows the progress of Brutus Jones, an African-American railroad porter who becomes dictator of a Caribbean island. O'Neill said his interest in the story came from the exploits of some actual rulers in Haiti. In the early nineteenth century, "President Sam" of Haiti claimed he could only be killed by a silver bullet. Sam, a former slave, made himself a chief in Haiti but committed suicide. Guillaume Sam, who followed him, was such a despot that he was hacked to death by his subjects.

O'Neill also read about tribal rituals in the Congo, where an accelerating drumbeat was used to raise a dancer's heart rate. Finally, O'Neill thought about his own expedition to South America in 1909–1910: "The effect of the tropical forest on the human imagination was honestly come by. It was the result of my own experience while prospecting for gold in Spanish Honduras."[11]

Because *The Emperor Jones* was innovative and technically challenging, O'Neill felt that Broadway producers might not be willing to finance it. The Provincetown Players, still led by Glaspell and Cook, were eager to try. Their goal was to create an expensive, radical "sky dome" for a set, and find a way to make characters such as Jones's "Little Formless Fears" and The Crocodile God appear on stage. In 1920, no African-American actor had ever played a leading role in a major white production. Charles S. Gilpin, who played bit parts and worked in African-American theater companies, was forty-one, muscular, and handsome. Among his many previous jobs, he had been a railroad porter. O'Neill said he was the perfect actor to play Jones.

> ### expressionism
>
> A style of artistic presentation that flourished in European theatre (as well as art) from about 1910 through the 1920s. Expressionism challenged materialist values and used distorted imagery to portray the human condition.

The black dialect written for Brutus Jones was counterbalanced by the Cockney dialect written for Smitty the trader. Caribbean natives spoke primitive English. Although the use of these dialects is extreme, O'Neill keeps each character consistent. Jones, who has escaped from a chain gang and become a powerful ruler over the natives, admits he is shrewd, greedy, and a confident showman. Gradually, Jones's regression into his subconscious fears and his past takes over when the natives turn on him. Visions of his chain gang, an American slave auction with planters and slaves, and tribal witch doctors and gods send Jones deeper into a state of terror. He ends up talking to himself and to the apparitions he perceives.

The natives, realizing Jones has stolen from them, plan his murder. Tribal leader Lem, whom O'Neill describes as "a

Charles Gilpin played the lead role in the Broadway production of *The Emperor Jones.*

heavy-set, ape-faced old savage of the extreme African type," directs his warriors to kill Jones.[12] Lem's speech sounds like poorly rendered American Indian dialect: "My mens dey got um silver bullets. Lead bullet no kill him. He got um strong charm. I cook um money, make um silver bullet, make um strong charm too."[13] Lem is one character who does not ring true.

The Emperor Jones opened on November 1, 1920, at 133 Macdougal Street, amazing critics and audiences with its radical concepts. Whether O'Neill really understood blacks and did not in some ways condescend to them is hard to say. How much he was influenced by Europe's expressionist movement in literature and art is also debatable. Regarding this play, O'Neill later claimed in 1926: "I had never heard of expressionism until long after the play was written. Its techniques grew naturally out of my own problems."[14]

Critics liked the experimental approach that started in European theatres and was now seen in O'Neill's work. Kenneth Macgowan, in his review for *Theatre Arts*, wrote: "These eight short scenes shake free from the traditional forms

CARL JUNG

O'Neill studied the writings of Swiss psychiatrist Carl Jung. Jung worked with Sigmund Freud from 1907–1912, but Freud disagreed over Jung's publication "The Psychology of the Unconscious." Jung stated people had universal archetypes or dispositions built into them at birth. Emperor Jones's traveling back through the collective racial experiences of black men reflected Jung's regression theories.

of our drama . . . in a study of personal and racial psychology of real imaginative truth."[15]

O'Neill was wrong about *The Emperor Jones* being too radical for Broadway. Producers were eager to buy it, giving it a successful 204-performance run starting on January 29, 1921. Charles Gilpin played Jones to great acclaim, although O'Neill had to watch carefully in case he changed some of his lines. One thing marred Gilpin's triumph: the New York Drama League did not invite him to their annual banquet for Broadway stars, due to his race. O'Neill protested, along with many leading actors. When the Drama League relented, and invited Gilpin in response, the banquet had its best attendance ever.

In her review of a 2006 revival of the play at Theatre La MaMa in New York, Glenda Frank wrote: "Brutus Jones carries the burden of black oppression within him, ghosts he can't exorcise. He is O'Neill's Macbeth, a man of promise and valor who is killed by the silver bullets that represent his greed and ambition."[16]

In a June 8, 1919, letter to Professor Baker at Harvard, O'Neill announced that he had landed a theatrical agent, who had sold his latest long play. O'Neill's self-destructive days were waning. He wrote constantly and productively, turning out short and long plays. With a group of one-acts being produced and published, plus *Beyond the Horizon* and one which would become *Anna Christie* on track for production, the end of 1919 found Eugene O'Neill finally off the paternal dole at age thirty. But the triumph O'Neill felt from *The Emperor Jones* was lessened by personal tragedy.

Soon after James O'Neill Sr. had seen the 1920 Broadway opening of *Beyond the Horizon*, he suffered a stroke. Doctors then discovered he had inoperable colon cancer, and he died on August 10, 1920, with Eugene, Ella, and Jamie attending him. Eugene's reaction to his father's death was to drown his depression by drinking. Jamie, amazingly, forced himself to abstain from alcohol for his mother's sake, and was able to assist at the funeral.

On a happier note, O'Neill's son Eugene Jr. re-entered his life. The boy's mother, Kathleen, had remarried when Eugene Jr. was five, so the boy regarded his stepfather as his parent. When Kathleen saw that O'Neill was making money, she asked if he would help educate his son. O'Neill had a meeting with the boy when his next play was in rehearsal in New York. The eleven-year-old in his military academy uniform greatly impressed O'Neill, who invited the boy to join him the following summer on Cape Cod with Agnes and their son, Shane. From then on, Eugene Jr. was a regular member of the O'Neill family.

naturalism

In art or literature, the philosophy of portraying ordinary people and life as it naturally is, without distortion or idealization.

symbol

Something that stands for, represents, or suggests another thing.

The Emperor Jones, along with *Beyond the Horizon*, made Eugene O'Neill America's most promising new playwright. His next full-length play, *Anna Christie*, was nearly ready and would open November 2, 1921.

Anna Christie was a return to naturalism. A full four acts, this work is set 1920 and concerns the relationship between a sailor father, his fallen daughter, her sailor suitor, and the sea. Often used by O'Neill as a symbol for the mysterious fate or destiny awaiting men, the sea is also a lure, a lifestyle, and a living for these characters. The natural element of fog plays a symbolic as well as naturalistic role.

Chris Christophersen is a strong but simple man from Sweden. Chris sent his young daughter to grow up with Minnesota farm relatives after her mother died. Convincing himself that Anna would be better off on land, yet knowing no other livelihood than that of a bosun (or boatswain, a ship's officer), Chris rarely sees Anna as she matures. He tells his drunken cronies that she is coming to join him. With his job as a barge captain, he feels he can keep tabs on his innocent daughter whom he believes is a nurse.

Anna Christie, arriving in the saloon when Chris is in the back room, confesses to Marthy, Chris's prostitute girlfriend, that she was raped and has been driven to a bad life. "It was men on the farm ordering and beating me—and giving me the wrong start. Then when I was a nurse, it was men again hanging around, bothering me, trying to see what they could get. And now it's men all the time. Gawd, I hate 'em all . . ."[17] As Chris takes Anna on his barge up the coast to Province-town, their relationship changes and deepens. She comes to trust him and to love the feel of the sea, even the enveloping fog. The water-borne life restores her spirit: "I feel clean, somehow—like you feel yust after you've took a bath. And I feel happy for once—yes, honest!"[18]

Mat Burke, a powerful young Irish seaman, enters Anna's life as the sea virtually coughs him up. Mat has survived a steamer wreck and instantly becomes attracted to Anna. The need and guilt O'Neill may have felt about using prostitutes is explored when Mat admits he has been a patron, but recoils to discover Anna has been forced to sell herself as well. The long, difficult road to understanding, self-discovery, forgiveness, and acceptance for Anna, Mat, and Chris makes up the conclusion of the play.

The creation of consistent voices, unique dialects, and distinct personalities for these divergent characters was an achievement of *Anna Christie*. Mat's Irish Catholic attitude about male and female roles reflects the dominant Irishmen O'Neill knew. Chris's confusion about a father's power and duty as he comes late to care for his child may reflect the realizations O'Neill was making as both a father and a son. The most complex character by far is Anna, who at age twenty, has a great deal to overcome. When she first appears, Anna is depressed, a hardened drinker. As she frankly tells her shocking story of abuse and survival, we start to care about her. However, in 1920, a woman who had been raped, became a prostitute, and could swear like a sailor did not make a sympathetic heroine. How Anna holds her own with her father and Mat and earns audience support is part of the magic O'Neill works with this character.

Critics praised *Anna Christie* as a rich, realistic, and salty work that grips the audience throughout. However, some complained that the last scenes were melodramatic and weakened the plot. Without knowing each others' plans, Chris and Mat sign on for a voyage on the same ship. Fate has led two men who distrust each other to be linked on a voyage. Anna finally convinces Mat that she hated all the men that had sex with her, begging him to accept her as reformed. Mat admits: "I'm thinking 'twasn't your fault, maybe, but having that old ape for a father that left you to grow up alone, made you what you was . . ."[19] When Anna swears on Mat's mother's crucifix that she will love only him and forget all the "badness" she has done, Mat relents and promises they will marry, for it is "the will of God."

Greta Garbo (far left) films a café scene from *Anna Christie* in 1930.

Although the critics admired the play's power, some questioned the resolution. O'Neill responded to the critics in the December 18, 1921, *New York Times*, writing that his goal was to have the audience leave with "a deep feeling of life flowing on, of the past which is never the past—but always the birth of the future . . ."[20] He noted that a kiss and a word about marriage might have made the audience blind to the play's real conclusion. Old Chris made "his gloomy, foreboding comment on the new set of coincidences, which to him reveal the old devil sea—(fate)—up to her old tricks again." Mat Burke "for the first time in the play, overcome by superstitious dread, agrees with the old man."[21] O'Neill said that although his characters have solved one crisis, they will go on to endure others.

When interviewed by Malcolm Mollan in 1922 about the play's ending, O'Neill claimed there was no ending at all. "The final curtain falls just as a new play is beginning . . . A naturalistic play is life. Life doesn't end. One experience is but the birth of another."[22]

Anna Christie brought Eugene O'Neill his second Pulitzer Prize. The play ran a season on Broadway, a year on the road plus a year in London, and became popular in stock and regional theatres. Hollywood turned out a successful silent film version starring Blanche Sweet, in spite of the play's depressing content. Gene and Aggie were financially blooming.

Confident that he was on track to continued success, O'Neill bought Brook Farm in Ridgefield, Connecticut. Gene and Aggie and the boys had their first real home.

But the pleasures of 1922 for O'Neill were balanced by the pain of losing his mother. Ella O'Neill had died from a stroke on February 28, 1922, while in Los Angeles, California. Jamie was with her. The moment Jamie saw his mother was dying, he started drinking again. O'Neill, involved in rehearsals of his new play, *The Hairy Ape*, fell into the kind of emotional paralysis that all serious crises caused for him. Both of his parents were gone. And he could not support or relate to his brother Jamie again.

Capitalism, Race, and Lust for Land: O'Neill Explores New Themes

"The throb of the drum in The Emperor Jones *cleared many a pair of ears that had been until that time tuned only to suburban comedy. The chesty roar of* The Hairy Ape *made several people forget to read how* The Well Dressed man *would wear his cravat."*

—John Dos Passos, in his 1925 essay "Is the Realistic Theatre Obsolete?"[1]

Eugene O'Neill's next drama, *The Hairy Ape*, was in rehearsal with the Provincetown Players when he had to cope with the loss of his mother and the collapse of his brother. It is a credit to O'Neill that he did manage Ella O'Neill's funeral at the Catholic church she had attended in New York City. With Aggie's help, he supervised her burial in New London, beside her husband, her infant son, and her mother. Despite his own grief and emotional stress over his play in progress, O'Neill gave his mother the traditional farewell she deserved. Jamie's retreat into alcohol was so deep that he could not participate in the funeral.

O'Neill admitted that he was confident enough to keep writing *The Hairy Ape* because he had already found the actor who could play the difficult leading role of Robert "Yank" Smith. Yank had to display powerful physical prowess, erratic emotional transitions, and deliver lengthy monologues, all with a perfect Brooklyn accent. Louis Wolheim, a friend of famed actors John and Lionel Barrymore, was presented to O'Neill—who saw in the ex-football player's pulverized face his perfect leading man. Well educated yet inexperienced as an actor, Wolheim grabbed his chance to become a star.

The Hairy Ape opened at the Greenwich Village home of the Provincetown Players on March 9, 1922. It would be their final Eugene O'Neill premiere. The playwright no longer needed the experimental workshop that had built his career; Broadway producers, impressed with his appeal to audiences, now asked for his new plays.

Like *The Emperor Jones*, *The Hairy Ape* has eight scenes, but it is longer and more complex. O'Neill stated it ran the gamut from extreme naturalism to expressionism. His goal was to tell the tale of an Everyman—a laborer who ended up at war with upper-class capitalist society.

Plot Challenges in a Unique Play: *The Hairy Ape*

The title character of *The Hairy Ape* is O'Neill's representative of the dispossessed, lower-class worker. Robert Smith, known as "Yank," is a stoker on a passenger ship. Yank is part of the flaming coal and steel world in which he lives. O'Neill describes the stokers using images of Neanderthal Man, "hairy chested, with long arms of tremendous power, and low, receding brow above their small, fierce resentful eyes."[2] Yank can also be seen as a figure in the study of evolution, a popular subject in the 1920s. He begins his tragic journey below the sea in a fiery core (the ship's furnace room) and emerges onto land (New York) as he evolves.

O'Neill's *The Hairy Ape* debuted on Broadway in 1922. The production starred Louis Wolheim and Carlotta Monterey.

The ship's stokers ridicule the wealthy elite passengers above them on deck. The socialist Cockney named Long calls them the "damned Capitalist Class."[3] Yank says about the men upstairs: "Put one of 'em down here for one watch in the stokehold, wha'd happen? Day'd carry him off on a stretcher . . . Who makes dis old tub run? Ain't it us guys? Well den, we belong and dey don't."[4] Yank is proud of his physical power and ability to perform a horrendous job.

In the second scene, the beautiful Mildred Douglas insists on visiting the men below. She is the "social activist" heiress of a steel empire. When she forces the officers to take her to the stokehold and sees the ferocious Yank bellowing vile curses at the engineer who drives him, Mildred is stunned. O'Neill describes her collapse from the "impact of this unknown, abysmal brutality, naked and shameless." As she stares at Yank's gorilla-like face, she says to the officers, "Take me away! Oh, the filthy beast!" and promptly faints.[5] Yank, realizing the depth of Mildred's insult, roars and hurls his coal shovel after the men who carry her off.

Furious, Yank would like to fling the heiress into the furnace, or beat in her face with a shovel. "She done me doit, didn't she? I'll get square with her! . . . I'll show her who's an ape!"[6] Suddenly the action moves to Fifth Avenue, New York City. Yank and Long, dressed in shore leave clothing, are searching for Mildred. Rich, elegant men and women, described as characterless marionettes, populate the avenue. When Yank bumps into them, they look straight through him. As a result of his behavior, Yank endures some police brutality and is thrown into prison on Blackwell's Island. The cage-like cells give the prison its nickname: The Zoo.

While in jail, a fellow prisoner reads Yank a newspaper article about the Industrial Workers of the World (IWW), claiming they are violent anarchists. As soon as he is released, Yank shows up at a local IWW office, a national socialist labor union that represents unskilled and low-paid workers. In the 1920s, the IWW favored slowdowns, boycotts, strikes, and even sabotage in order to fight for better working conditions. Yank will join the IWW if they help destroy Mildred's father's mills: "blow up the factory, de woiks, where he makes de steel . . . knock all de steel in de woild up to de moon. Dat'll fix tings!"[7] The IWW leaders fear that Yank has been sent by the government to entrap them. One calls Yank "a brainless ape" and has the other members throw him out.

Lost and confused about his place in the world, Yank wanders to the city zoo and finds the ape house. His final monologue is delivered to the gorilla caged there. Yank comes to a tragic conclusion. He realizes Mildred feared him as an uncaged beast. "She woon't wise dat I was in a cage too—worser'n yours—sure—a . . . sight—'cause you got some chanct to bust loose—but me . . ."[8] Prying open the gorilla's cage, Yank sets him free and extends his hand: "Shake—the secret grip of our order." Overwhelmed with his new freedom, the gorilla crushes Yank's body with a hug, throws him into the cage full of chattering apes, and leaves him to die of his injuries. O'Neill's final stage direction muses: "And perhaps *The Hairy Ape* at last belongs."[9]

Where in contemporary mechanized society does a humble laborer like Yank belong? This is the central dilemma explored in *The Hairy Ape*. O'Neill had discovered expressionism, as he later explained: "the whole play is expressionistic. Yank is really yourself and myself. He is every human being."[10]

O'Neill manages wonderfully to capture the voices, dialects, attitudes, and interactions of these varied characters from all classes—from the wealthy to the union bosses to the manual laborers. They step right out of real-life situations, even if they are intended to be more symbolic. O'Neill appreciated the way one of his favorites, Swedish playwright August Strindberg, turned characters into symbols, although he avoided doing this as obviously. He preferred to keep his characters more believable, so the audience would relate to them and absorb their ideas and meanings.

Louis Wolheim played the role of Yank Smith in both the Greenwich Village and Broadway productions. Robert Dowling stated that Wolheim was perfect because "he regularly associated with people like Yank and could handily reproduce the Brooklyn workingman's persona."[11] Wolheim's ability to transform himself into Yank kept audiences transfixed and the box office humming. Carlotta Monterey, an elegant actress who would come to play a much larger role in O'Neill's life, portrayed Mildred on Broadway.

Critics differed on what *The Hairy Ape* achieved and whether it was too much of a socialist treatise. Those who liked the play included Robert Benchley of *Life*, who called it O'Neill's most powerful work yet, and Alexander Woollcott of the *New York Times*, who said it was uneven, but "O'Neill towers about the milling mumbling crowd of contemporary playwrights."[12] The *New York Tribune*'s critic declared "O'Neill is a young genius and our greatest playwright, completely lacking in superficiality."[13]

Mired in Racial Intolerance: *All God's Chillun Got Wings*

All God's Chillun Got Wings was written in the fall of 1923 in Provincetown, while O'Neill's brother Jamie was dying of acute alcoholism in New Jersey. Estranged from his family, Jamie died from a stroke in a sanatorium on November 8, 1923, at age forty-five. Eugene fell into a depression and bouts of drinking, haunted by his dead brother and their broken relationship. His wife, Agnes, and her sister were forced to make the arrangements for Jamie's funeral service and burial in New London. Eugene said he was too ill to attend (he did have the flu). He immersed himself in writing *All God's Chillun Got Wings*, which was intended to be a short play for publication in *American Mercury* magazine. The subjects of the play were both interracial bigotry and marital relations.

Set in the Lower East Side where black and white neighborhoods meet, *All God's Chillun* spans sixteen years in the lives of Jim, an African-American boy, and Ella, a lower-class white girl. Ella's lifelong fondness for Jim stops when they graduate from high school and she picks up the racist attitudes of her Irish boyfriends. Jim's black friends resent him for his "white" goals of college and law school. After five years pass, Ella has a child out of wedlock who dies of diphtheria. Thrown out by her Irish family, Ella tells Jim: "You've been the only one in the world who's stood by me—the only understanding person—and all after the rotten way I used to treat you . . . you've been white to me, Jim."[14] Jim tells her, "All love is white. I've always loved you." Ella, destitute and lonely, agrees to marry Jim. He vows to devote his life to her.

In Act Two, two years later, Jim's mother and sister await the couple's return from abroad. Interracial marriage was more accepted in Europe than America at that time. Ella begins to have an emotional breakdown. Jim resumes his drive to pass the bar exam. When Jim's sister begs him to commit Ella, who has declined into a pathetic, bigoted child, he says: "She's all I've got! You with your fool talk of the black race and the white race! Where does the human race get a chance to come in?"[15] In the final act, Ella takes infantile

SHOCK OF INTERRACIAL MARRIAGE

In the 1920s, black male-white female marriage was rare and startling, even in New York. An exception was Jack Johnson, the first black world-champion boxer, who made public his love for white women. He married Etta Duryea, a white woman who committed suicide in 1912, perhaps in response to Johnson's abuse. Johnson married another white woman, Lucille Cameron, later that year. He had married two more white women by 1925. O'Neill reflected some of the public anger caused by Jack Johnson's marriages.

pleasure in Jim's failure to pass the bar again. She kisses his hand, begging him to never leave her. Four times Jim and Ella express their exclusion from society as they say, "you're all I've got." Jim swears to care for Ella "up to the gates of Heaven."

Jim Harris and Ella Downey shared first names with James and Ella O'Neill. The roller-coaster nature of the O'Neills' emotional relations can be seen in their namesakes. Ella O'Neill's tendency to isolate herself, feeling cut off from friends and family due to her marriage, is reflected in Ella Downey. O'Neill said he intended the play to be about the tragedy of all prejudice, saying Jim Harris could have been Jewish, Turkish, Japanese—any race that was discriminated against by white Christian society.

A powerful young black actor named Paul Robeson played Jim Harris. The respected leading lady of the Provincetown Players, Mary Blair, portrayed Ella. This time Robeson and Blair, as well as O'Neill, were in for trouble when the published play preceded the production. Many people were shocked and

Paul Robeson and Flora Robson starred in the 1928 film *All God's Chillun Got Wings.*

angered to learn *All God's Chillun* was about intermarriage and that the white wife actually kisses her black husband's hand. In spite of death threats, the play opened on Macdougal Street on May 26, 1924, and ran for its scheduled one hundred performances.

Due to a mixed reception from the New York critics, who said it was too full of exposition and affectation, the play never received a Broadway production. One of O'Neill's usual fans, critic Alexander Woollcott, said that the love between Jim and Ella was a "highly improbable situation in the first place."[16] Clearly this play arrived before its time.

Another problem with the play may have been O'Neill's tendency to move into stereotype with both the black and the Irish characters. In order for the play to reach true tragic stature, we must essentially believe in Jim Harris and Ella Downey and in the assumptions they are fed by their families. Some critics like Michael Manheim contend the O'Neill's characters can stand in for other racial and religious minorities. Edward Shaunessy writes that "because they breathe and interact in a culture of sickness, both Jim and Ella even as children have been infected by America's most lethal virus: racism."[17]

Jordan Miller wrote: "*All God's Chillun* remains an original and important experiment. . . . The reactions of a racially mixed couple whose lives are torn asunder psychologically rather than physically by the traditions of a segregated society are perceptively dramatized." He praised the emotional catharsis through "Jim's heroic acceptance of an inevitable fate."[18]

Family Triangle Shattered by Lust:
Desire Under the Elms

Desire Under the Elms became O'Neill's first attempt to recreate an American story in the form of a Greek tragedy. Written early in 1924, it blends several tragic story lines from Greek theatre and mythology. *Oedipus Rex* by Sophocles tells the story of a young ruler who kills a man he does not realize is his father, then falls in love with and weds his own mother. *Hippolytus* by Euripedes is the story of the son of Theseus. When Hippolytus denies the desires of the goddess Aphrodite, she puts lust in the heart of Hippolytus and his stepmother Phaedra, who commits suicide in despair over her hopeless love for her stepson. *Medea*, also by Euripedes, tells the tale of a princess and sorceress who falls in love with Jason. Medea aids Jason in regaining the Golden Fleece and marries him in his kingdom of Iolcos. After Medea, Jason, and their two children are exiled to Corinth, Jason turns away from Medea. When Jason marries the princess of Corinth, Medea in a jealous fury murders her two children by Jason.

Elements of these three Greek tragedies can be seen woven into *Desire Under the Elms*. The relationship triangle of the play's aging father, his angry son, and the father's newly acquired young wife, is set on an 1850 New England farm. The original set by Robert Edmond Jones was based on O'Neill's own sketch. The open exterior walls of the farmhouse allow the audience to see into the kitchen, parlor, father's bedroom, and son's bedroom. It symbolizes the external natural world of the farmland, vs. the convoluted inner world of the house's residents. Ephraim, the father, cleared the stones from his fields and used them for a wall which surrounds the house, locking the trio in together. Two enormous elms bow over the roof, shielding them from the prying eyes of the world.

O'Neill was determined to be blunt about the physical, emotional, and sexual lives of the three protagonists, even if his play was criticized or banned. By using a farm locale, O'Neill made it more natural for the characters to use earthy language and animal metaphors. O'Neill wrote out the dialect of rural New England slang and pronunciation.

The action follows the desires of Ephraim Cabot, the seventy-six-year-old patriarch, his new bride and third wife Abbie, and his youngest son Eben, who is still attached to his mother and burning with a need to "revenge" her death. Ephraim claims to be a devout Christian and often quotes from the Bible, but he is a heartless father and self-absorbed man. His physical needs and his passion for his cows and his land are all that count to him. His two older sons, Simeon and Peter (both from Ephraim's first wife), realize when their father comes home with Abbie that they are unlikely to inherit the farm. Eben finds out about his father's hidden money and buys out his brothers' shares, bidding them goodbye. Abbie's powerful drive to make the farm her own stuns Eben, who fears the farm may go to her when his father dies. Abbie and Eben's friction over the land turns to lust. Their desire drives them to thwart Ephraim, a man they have come to hate. When Abbie gets pregnant by Eben, she passes the baby off as Ephraim's son. Their motives shift, until desire forces Abbie to kill her own baby to prove that she did not get pregnant just to possess the farm. Logic and reason evaporate, until at the end passion for the land and for one another has destroyed the pair.

Scholar Doris Alexander pointed out that when Abbie's seduction of Eben turns to love, and Eben rejects her, "she proves her greater love for him by killing the baby she loves.

Out of the magnitude of her sacrifice for love, she rises to tragic exaltation."[19]

Ephraim understands his two older sons because they relate to the farm and the livestock. About his youngest, Ephraim says: "Eben's a dumb fool—like his Maw—soft and simple!"[20] When Simeon and Peter take off, Ephraim says: "Lord God o' Hosts, smite the undutiful sons with Thy wust cuss."[21] Eben says to hell with his father's God who does nothing but deliver curses. The impasse between Ephraim and Eben never lessens, as Ephraim belittles his son by insisting he is still worth ten of him.

In a long monologue, Ephraim explains to Abbie how he had remained strong and hard, like the stones he has laboriously cleared and piled into walls. "God's hard, not easy! God's in the stones!" he tells Abbie.[22] Ephraim also feels the chill in the house emanating from the ghost of Eben's mother. Once Ephraim believes that Abbie's baby is his son, he feels new power. Telling Eben about Abbie's plans to cut him out of the farm, Ephraim nearly chokes Eben. When Abbie separates them, Ephraim shouts: "Seventy-six and him not thirty yit—an' look whar he be fur thinking his Paw was easy! No, by God, I hain't easy. An' him upstairs, I'll raise him to be like me."[23]

After Abbie commits her terrible infanticide, Ephraim tells her that he knew something unnatural was happening in the house, driving him to the beasts in the barn. "I'll live to a hundred," he tells her. "I'll live to see ye hung. I'll deliver up the jedgment o' God an' the law."[24] Later, he breaks down and tells Abbie that if she had loved him, he would have never told the Sheriff on her, no matter what. He ends "lonesomer'n ever."[25]

Abbie Cabot, a poor thirty-five-year-old country woman in the nineteenth century, knows she has few options for a better life. She grabs a chance for a farm of her own by marrying Ephraim. Abbie realizes she has a fierce competitor for the land in Eben. Although her longing for the younger son starts to consume her, Abbie still needs to stay in control. When Eben heads off to visit the village prostitute, she yells at him: "Ye're only livin' here 'cause I tolerate ye! Git along! I hate the sight o' ye!"[26] When Ephraim tells Abbie she could have anything she wanted if she gave him a son, her desire to have her home and security overcomes all else. However, her need for Eben drives her back into his arms. O'Neill describes their first sexual encounter, then says: "They stand speechless and breathless, panting like two animals."[27] Soon Eben courts Abbie in the front parlor, the sanctuary of his mother's ghost. As Abbie seduces Eben, their hatred and lust combine to explode into a perverse relationship.

Abbie's love for Eben drives her to deceive Ephraim. She breaks down and begs for Eben's love—the only real joy she has ever had. Believing Eben threatened to leave because of the son he perceives will now inherit the farm, Abbie kills the baby. As Eben leaves to get the sheriff to arrest her, she calls after him: "I don't care what ye do—if ye'll only love me agen" and faints.[28]

Eben Cabot's character has been shaped by a lifelong conflict with his father and a near idolatry of his dead mother. Not as physically strong or in touch with the livestock as his brothers, Eben wants to run the farm mainly out of revenge. His role seems to be the weakling and loser, torn between avenging his mother, triumphing over his father, and possessing his stepmother. This Oedipal conflict was seldom displayed so boldly in American drama. As the play progresses, we see Eben become less of a reactor and more of a man capable of love. By the play's end, he owns up to his part as Abbie's lover and deserter. Eben tells the sheriff that he

The O'Neills (left to right: Eugene, Agnes, Oona, and Shane) pose for a family portrait in Bermuda around 1925.

helped her: "You kin take me, too."[29] The land they fought over and desired is the last thing they see together.

By taking ancient Greek myths and blending them perfectly into an American family's lives, this play "established him as a dramatist of true genius and is the culmination of the first period of composition.[30] *Desire Under the Elms* was strong material for 1924. The Manhattan district attorney threatened to prosecute the producers for indecency, although nothing obscene actually happened onstage. The play was banned in Boston, and not all the New York critics felt it was a complete success. However, it enjoyed a 208-performance run on Broadway after it had made a hit in Greenwich Village. It went on to become the first of O'Neill's plays to receive regular revivals around the country.

On May 14, 1925, Eugene and Aggie welcomed daughter Oona, who joined five-year-old Shane. Although O'Neill was writing prolifically, he was also falling back into depressions and alcoholism. As he worked on the scenarios for his next major works, *Lazarus Laughed* and *Strange Interlude*, O'Neill realized he needed medical and psychiatric help to conquer his recurring lapses into mental illness and addiction.

O'NEILL EXAMINES THE HUMAN PSYCHE VS. MODERN VALUES THE GREAT GOD BROWN, MARCO MILLIONS, LAZARUS LAUGHED, AND STRANGE INTERLUDE

"*Success is still our only real living religion.*"

—Eugene O'Neill, writing to Richard Dana Skinner[1]

In 1925 Eugene O'Neill saw his country, perhaps all of the western world, heading toward massive expansion and endless material abundance. The Roaring Twenties might have been almost enjoyable for O'Neill when he was young. But at age thirty-seven and a father of three, he saw what was happening to society as almost a biblical curse. His own father, James O'Neill, spoke to him from his death bed, telling him he was going on to a better life: "this sort of life here—all froth—no good"[2] His father's words made O'Neill determined to rethink modern values, and explore the present times in his work.

In a prolific stint of writing, Eugene turned out four major plays in just three years. *The Great God Brown* and *Marco Millions* were written in 1925, and *Lazarus Laughed* and

NIETZSCHE JOINS FREUD AS INFLUENTIAL THINKER

O'Neill studied Sigmund Freud and philosopher Friedrich Nietzsche throughout 1925. Freud's theories on depression, repression, and the influence of the subconscious on human behavior impressed him. Nietzsche, a German author of political and critical philosophy, promoted life affirmation and reliance on animal instincts. He was opposed to traditional Christianity, saying that it did not appreciate our present life and focused too much on evil, repression, and death. Nietzsche developed severe physical and mental illness in his forties, probably due to syphilis and its treatment drug, mercury, and died by 1900.

Strange Interlude were completed in 1926 and 1927. The last of these has remained an innovative, highly regarded work.

The Great God Brown: A Mixed, Bewildering Success

The Great God Brown, produced by Provincetown Playhouse regulars Kenneth Macgowan and designer/director Robert Edmond Jones, opened at the Greenwich Village theatre in January 1926. O'Neill demanded that the cast perform with various masks that they put on and removed constantly. Often characters did not recognize one another when unmasked. Different aspects of their personalities emerged as they masked and unmasked. Realism gave way to levels of mysticism. O'Neill had watched his parents and brother assume one face onstage, one face in public, one face in private, and one secret face known only to themselves. Masks revealed to the audience various elements of a character's personality and emotion, as well as the layers of the person's subconscious.

O'Neill was very interested in the theories of Sigmund Freud, an Austrian doctor and the father of psychoanalysis.

O'Neill later stated that "I still consider this play one of the most interesting and moving I have written. It has its faults . . . but it does succeed in conveying a sense of the tragic mystery of Life . . . and this is the true test of whether any play, however excellent its structure . . . is true drama or just another play."[3]

The Great God Brown was so unusual in its approach that audience members who saw it in Greenwich Village were confused. As *The Great God Brown* moved to Broadway in March, O'Neill printed an "explanation" in the newspapers to help audiences understand his methods and meaning. Although use of the masks and constant alterations in character were exhausting to the actors, the performers made it work.

Two families and their relationships make up the core of *The Great God Brown*. We meet William "Billy" Brown and Dion Anthony as they are graduating from high school. Both are deeply attracted to classmate Margaret. Dion's name is short for Dionysus, the Greek god of wine, dance, and celebration of life. Billy is the grounded, solid guy who develops into a successful architect-contractor. Dion marries Margaret, goes through his family money, and becomes a suffering, confused failure. Margaret treats him as an impractical child who does not function well in the working world. When masked, O'Neill describes Dion as "dark, spiritual, poetic, passionately super-sensitive."[4] When unmasked, Dion is "shy and gentle, full of a deep sadness."[5]

We meet Cybel, a prostitute, when Dion ends up drunk in her parlor. Cybel's name is similar to Sibyl, in Greek

realism

An approach in playwriting to present characters and situations as they would appear in real life.

mythology an oracle or seer who also attracts men. When unmasked, Cybel is kind and motherly, but when masked she becomes a hard-hearted prostitute who says, "when you got to love to live, it's hard to love living."[6]

Dion recalls his relationship with his own father and mother: "I wondered where I had met that man before. Only at the second of my conception. After that, we grew hostile with concealed shame. And my mother? I remember a sweet, strange girl, with affectionate, bewildered eyes as if God had locked her in a dark closet without any explanation. I was the sole doll our ogre, her husband, allowed her, and she played mother and child with me for many years."[7] This speech calls up psychological problems that O'Neill suffered with his own father and mother. Due to Margaret's begging, Billy Brown offers Dion a draftsman's job in his office. Dion coins the phrase "The Great God Brown" when Billy's offer of employment saves his family.

Seven years later, we find Dion still lounging in Cybel's parlor, where both play solitaire. Dion's Pan-like mask has changed into Mephistopheles. This character-mask symbolizes the fallen angel, the one that legend says was banished from heaven after Lucifer, and has powers to corrupt others. Cybel becomes the caring prostitute who says: "I'm so damn sorry for the lot of you, every damn mother's son-of-a-gun that I'd like to run out naked into the street and love the whole mob to death like I was bringing you all a new brand of dope that'd make you forget everything that ever was for good!"[8] Dion announces that the doctor has told him he will have a heart attack unless he stops drinking, which he cannot find the strength to do.

As Dion loses his sanity and his heart fails, his mask falls. O'Neill describes his real face as a Christian martyr's at the point of death—a strange transition from Mephistopheles and Dionysus to a Christ-figure. Dion wills Margaret's love to Billy, then dies. Billy takes Dion's mask, and assumes his role. Somehow, he plays both men. A bizarre monologue with Billy talking to Dion's mask tells us that he is drinking in Dion's life force. Margaret accepts Brown/Dion as her lover, her husband, and her big boy, saying "you've become quite human—like me—and I'm so happy, dear."[9]

Later, Dion's alcoholism and passions possess Billy, who, when playing Dion, described himself as "soused on life."[10] The characters move back and forth until it appears "Dion" has killed off the personality of "Billy Brown." Billy portraying Dion makes his way to Cybel's, where police shoot him. As he dies, he says: "The laughter of Heaven sows Earth with a rain of tears, and out of Earth's transfigured birth-pain the laughter of Man returns to bless and play again in innumerable dancing gales of flame upon the knees of God."[11]

Although the constant shifting of roles and masks and symbols challenged audiences' comprehension, *The Great God Brown* was so intriguing that the play had a solid run of 283 performances. Critics struggled to understand this great experiment. Brooks Atkinson, the young critic for the *New York Times*, admitted that the play was often unclear. Patiently Atkinson explains that O'Neill's strength is "his absorption in the ideal as opposed to the practical."[12] The symbolism, psychological analysis, and dialogue turned to poetry caused some critics to claim it was O'Neill at his best and his worst. *Drama Magazine* said it represented the highest development of O'Neill's genius. Joseph Wood Krutch in the *Nation* noted that the playwright "is himself too close to the passions with which he is dealing to objectify them completely, and they master him quite as often as he is able to master them."[13]

Marco Millions: O'Neill's Satire on Capitalism

Marco Millions, the first O'Neill play to be produced by the Theatre Guild, opened in New York in 1928. It received mixed reviews and had just ninety-two performances. Three actors—Alfred Lunt, Morris Carnovsky, and Sanford Meisner—all became major figures in the American theatre. But even Lunt's portrait of Marco Polo, as he encounters Kublai the Great Khan during the Renaissance, was not enough to make the play work. Most audiences found the enormous cast, divided into "Christians" and "Heathens," overwhelming. Although the spectacle was brilliant, the eleven scenes spread throughout Persia, Venice, India, Mongolia, Cathay, Xanadu, and Cambulac proved far too demanding to follow or absorb. The satiric concept of comparing Marco Polo to a twentieth-century businessman floated over most people's heads.

Some critics appreciated the poetry and beauty in *Marco Millions*, but many failed to catch the irony O'Neill intended. Robert Coleman in the *New York Mirror* said the play was "amusing, heart-breaking, blending humor and grim drama, sympathetic and ironic. Prose soars to meet poetry."[14] However, O'Neill's strictest critic, Alexander Woollcott, in the *New York World* wrote: "The Babbitt theme is now a little worn; this is an elaborate way of saying the same thing."[15] Other critics agreed that authors like 1920s novelist Sinclair

---

Theatre Guild

An organization begun in 1919 to introduce new authors and produce radical works by Europeans and Americans.

---

satire

A dark style of comedy that not only makes us laugh but also reveals the hypocrisy and pretentiousness of our society.

Lewis had done a better job with the same subject: the spiritually bankrupt American capitalist seeking truth in the modern world.

Lazarus Laughed: But Few Others Did

Lazarus Laughed, a long four-act play, was also immensely difficult to produce. It is a fascinating revision of Biblical history and the character of Lazarus, raised from the dead by Jesus. With twelve major roles, nine choruses, and many crowd scenes, this drama included the use of masks. O'Neill wanted them designed to reflect the seven "ages of life." He referred to William Shakespeare's *As You Like It*, where the seven stages are listed as infant, school-boy, lover, soldier, businessman, elder, and second childhood into oblivion. O'Neill also wanted his many character or personality types to be divided by a dominant costume color. Obviously, this play would cost a fortune to stage. Therefore, its only production was by a theatre in Pasadena, California, in April 1928, where a massive group of volunteer actors and technicians staged the play. It never reached Broadway.

This tale of the capture and crucifixion of Christ presents Lazarus, who is revered as a god because he actually returned from the dead, telling his followers not to fear Death. "You forget the God in you," he says.[16] The Roman rulers distrust the cult of Lazarus. Tiberius actually murders Lazarus's wife, Miriam, to prove to Lazarus that Death does exist. In destroying Miriam, Tiberius also murders True Love, allowing Lust to survive. A sick, vicious ruler, Tiberius hated his mother and hardened himself to become Caesar. Eventually, the mad Emperor Caligula kills Lazarus and tells the mobs: "I have killed God! I am Death! Death is Caesar!"[17] The crowd becomes a bunch of terrified rats, squeaking: "Hail

Alfred Lunt starred as Marco in the original 1928 Broadway production of *Marco Millions*, which received mixed reviews.

to Death." In the final scene, the meaning of the play vacillates, as Lazarus assures Caligula there is no Death, only Laughter. The California critics were sufficiently intrigued to recommend the play to their Pasadena fans, but it went no further.

Strange Interlude: O'Neill's "Novel" on Fractured Personality

Strange Interlude was O'Neill's most ambitious work so far. At nine acts and two hundred pages, the play would run five hours. His own experience with psychoanalysis prompted O'Neill to present characters who interacted with one another in a normal, socially acceptable way—but also revealed inner responses from a hidden, repressed level. This new kind of "aside" was not just an out-of-character quip directed at the audience, but a verbal expression of the subconscious. O'Neill expected actors to move continually from interior to exterior modes of self-expression. Never having been a proficient actor himself, he did not understand how difficult it would be to maintain a consistent character while doing this. He also disregarded the dizzying effort demanded of an audience to follow this kind of emoting for five hours.

During 1926, O'Neill worked on *Strange Interlude*, both in Bermuda and in Belgrade Lakes, Maine. He had discovered he wrote well only when he was warm and able to swim, but fell into depressions during cold dark winters. Although wife Agnes and children Shane and Oona were with O'Neill most of the time, his heart was elsewhere. When Agnes took the children back to Bermuda, Eugene stayed on in New York and began an affair with Carlotta Monterey. His feelings for Agnes and Carlotta tore him in two. On December 15, 1926, Eugene wrote to Carlotta: "As soon as I reached here [Bermuda], I told Agnes exactly how I had felt about leaving you. I said I loved you. I also said, and with equal truth, that I loved her. Does this sound idiotic to you? I hope not!"[18]

Naturally, Agnes exploded with anger over what looked like the end of her difficult life with Gene. However, friends of the couple often said the marriage had broken down long ago, even before Oona was born. The stress was mainly due to alcoholism. The only time he contained his drinking, O'Neill confessed, was when he went on a writing binge.[19]

O'Neill wrote to Carlotta in February 1927: "This play, *Strange Interlude*—and it is really two plays, being nine acts in all—I feel as if something inside of me were writing about something inside the lives of people that gets beyond any of the usual psychological evaluations. I seem to hit on things that, dramatically at least, have never been touched before."[20] He ends by asking Carlotta if she really loves him, because he wants her in his life. On March 4, O'Neill wrote to Carlotta to tell her that the draft of *Strange Interlude* was finished. He claimed that there was no character in it "who, as 'Dion' in *Brown*, or a number of my characters, partly reproduces phases of my character or experience."[21] The characters were taken from "many men" that O'Neill knew.

By April 1927, O'Neill was writing love letters to Carlotta (in Europe) and "my own Aggie" in Bermuda, missing her, saying if he lost her love, he'd go mad with grief.[22] He spent most of 1927 rewriting *Strange Interlude* while often separated from both women. As he revised and crystallized the characters in *Strange Interlude*, O'Neill explored what he knew of women—and probably some aspects of his own fractured personality.

O'Neill's goal was to write a novel in play form, something he called a "novel-play." His plan was to chart the outer and inner life of a woman from age twenty through age forty-five.

The plot revolves around the Leeds family and the Evans family. We meet Professor Henry Leeds, who teaches classical literature at a small college. O'Neill perhaps used Connecticut College near his summer home in New London as a model. Leeds lives with his twenty-year-old daughter Nina, to whom he is possessively attached. The action begins in 1920, shortly after the end of World War I. Nina is still grieving over the loss of her fiancé Gordon Shaw in the war. Henry Leeds's younger friend, author Charles Marsden, is so close to him and to Nina that he is almost a member of the Leeds family group. The Evans family consists of Sam Evans, once a college classmate of Nina's fiancé, and his mother. The Evanses are farmers from upstate New York. These two families unite when Nina marries Sam, a good but ineffective man who sincerely loves her. Nina marries mainly because she has lost her true love, but believes motherhood will fulfill her.

After their marriage, Nina becomes pregnant with Sam's child. Mrs. Evans drops a bombshell by telling Nina that Sam's father and grandfather died insane, and one mad aunt is still living in the attic. The reality of this inherited mental illness (that seems to have skipped Sam's generation) has been kept a secret from Sam. When Mrs. Evans discovers Nina is pregnant, she urges Nina to abort this baby secretly, and somehow find a way to have a healthy baby and convince Sam that it is his. Abortion was legal but difficult in 1920, leaving Nina with a hard choice. After getting the abortion, she has to find a man willing to father a child. Dr. Edmund Darrell, who was attracted to Nina when she volunteered at his hospital before her marriage, seems the perfect sperm donor.

At age twenty-three, Nina bears a son who is the result of her sexual encounter with Edmund. Nina and Edmund develop a passion for each other, although Nina never divorces

Sam for fear it would destroy him. The son, named for Nina's dead fiancé Gordon, is eleven years old before he realizes his mother is emotionally involved with Edmund. Young Gordon and his supposed father, Sam, are extremely close.

The plot jumps forward another ten years to son Gordon's college years as he rows crew on the Hudson River and has a fiancé named Madeline Arnold. In her mid-forties, Nina is jealous of her son's relationship with Sam and with the lovely Madeline. Nina is obsessed with keeping Gordon unmarried and tied to her. Charles, who has lost the women he truly loved—his mother and sister—now understands what has transpired in Nina's emotional life. He knew her father Henry, her first love Gordon, her husband Sam, her lover Edmund, and now her son—and what she gave and took from all of them. At the end of the play, after Sam has died of a stroke and Gordon and Madeline are wed, Nina regresses back to her dependence on a father-figure, with Charles assuming this paternal role.

Nina Leeds is the focal character in *Strange Interlude*. O'Neill heard a story when living on Cape Cod about a woman whose fiancé was shot down just before the end of World War I. She became neurotic and desperate, prone to drinking and having affairs. O'Neill heard that she married without love, hoping motherhood would bring her a contented life. He wrote in his notebook that he wanted Nina's "thinking aloud" to be more important than her actual speeches to others. O'Neill pictured Nina as a confused, modern woman, obsessed with finding her power and personhood through relationships with men, hiding her private pain and desire.

While Nina gives herself emotionally and sexually to some of the veterans at the hospital where she volunteers, she is drawn to Dr. Edmund Darrell. Too career-driven to bother with marriage, Edmund makes a "prescription"—that Nina marry Sam Evans, who will father her child. Scholar Doris Alexander described this as a "fatal prescription,"[23] just as the morphine prescribed for O'Neill's mother, Ella, proved so damaging to her existence.

Nina marries Sam, but uses Edmund to give her sexual fulfillment and a healthy baby. Focusing her entire life force on her son, Nina avoids letting the boy take the journey into independent adulthood. She thinks aloud: "These men make me sick! I hate all three of them . . . the wife and mistress in me has been killed by them . . . thank God, I am only a mother now . . . Gordon is my little man."[24]

After Sam dies, and his son Gordon says he hopes that his mother Nina and Edmund can find happiness together, Nina wonders if she does not have to possess someone to have their real love.

Charles Marsden becomes the commentator on Nina Leeds and her men. Charles reflects much ambivalence about his work and about his role as a celibate man. Through the years, Charles tries to be a support for Nina, but his deepest love is for his mother and sister. Charles often helps the audience analyze the other characters around him. When he starts to see the carnal, sensual side of Nina, he is repelled and backs away from it. After Professor Leeds dies, Charles becomes a confidant of Sam Evans. Even Edmund speaks frankly in front of him. His suspicions are seen when Edmund prescribes marriage for Nina, wondering if the doctor is already her lover. He says aloud to Edmund in a joking tone: "Do you know what I'm inclined to suspect, Doctor? That you may be in love with Nina yourself!"[25]

At the end, Charles happily becomes the poet who will shelter Nina: "My life gathers roses, cooly crimson, in sheltered gardens, on late afternoons in love with evening . . . my life is an evening . . . Nina is my rose, exhausted by the long, hot day, leaning wearily toward peace."[26]

Sam Evans, with his farming background and his friendship with the noble Gordon Shaw, is a perfect choice for Nina's husband. Sam is slow and took much support to make it professionally in advertising. Charles believes he represents the "typical terrible child of the age . . . universal slogan, keep moving, moving where? Never mind that . . . the means are the end . . . keep moving!"[27] Sam's main motivation is raising the baby Gordon.

Edmund, doctor and scientist, moves in and out of the twenty-five-year span of Nina's life. Never married, always ambitious for fame, Edmund changes near the end, almost declares himself Gordon's father after Sam has died, then lets Gordon's love for Sam continue unblemished.

Gordon Evans is a remarkably perceptive boy. Handsome, likable, a good sport, Gordon tells his fiancé, Madeline, "I've always felt she [Nina] cared a lot for—Darrell. I've felt it too strongly."[28] He believed she fell for Dr. Edmund Darrell after her marriage and then sent him away: "He fought it down, too, on account of his friendship for Dad."[29]

What brings happiness and satisfaction in the modern family? What makes a woman choose one man and yet love another? When does acting on the truth in a family do more harm than good? Can we rely on religion to support us? O'Neill asks more questions than even a two-hundred-page play can answer. How other people influence our behavior and psychology is a primary theme. Nina's father and fiancé both died, yet their influence on her haunts her. Sam's grandfather and father, afflicted with a genetic disorder, seem to influence him very little. At age eleven, after seeing his mother

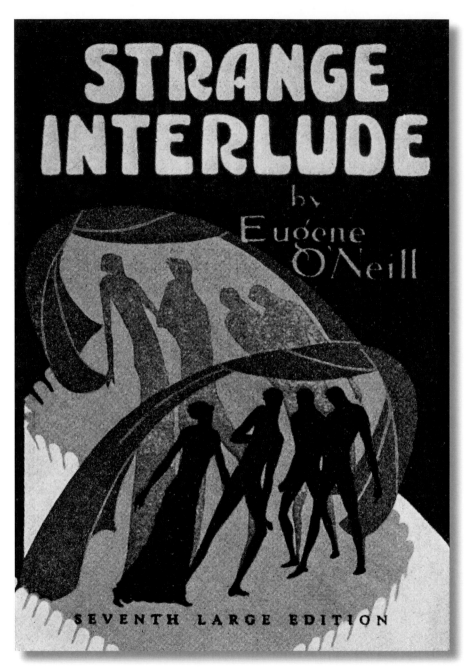

O'Neill won his third and final Pulitzer Prize for *Strange Interlude*, which was published in 1928.

kiss Dr. Edmund Darrell, Gordon turns against Nina—until he later realizes she has sacrificed her needs to be a faithful wife. Edmund is influenced by Sam's power over Nina and Gordon, even after Sam's death. When Sam leaves Edmund a financial settlement to support his research lab, the doctor thinks: "God . . . Sam! Wasn't it enough for him to own my wife, my son, in his lifetime? . . . now in death he reaches out to steal Preston! [Edmund's protégé in the lab] . . . to steal my work!"[30]

Charles and Nina discuss the term "strange interlude" during the final scene of the play. Charles tells Nina to forget the men in her life, calling her passionate existence a distressing episode, an interlude of trial and preparation. She replies: "Strange interlude. Yes, our lives are merely strange dark interludes in the electrical display of God the Father."[31] Nina rests, contented but weary with life.

O'Neill wrote to his wife Agnes on Christmas 1927 and brought his marriage to a close: "I love someone else. Most deeply. There is no possible doubt of this. And the someone loves me."[32] Although he wanted to be friends, he would not live with Agnes again and filed for divorce.

Strange Interlude opened in New York on January 30, 1928. Some called it a long-winded, sordid mess. Others said it was a magnificent venture, "cleaving the skyline of tomorrow."[33] Percy Hammond of the *New York Herald-Tribune* summed it up, saying the play "contains everything but brevity to make it an exciting evening in the theatre."[34] Nicholas Dudley of the *New York World* went further: "O'Neill catches not only a life but life itself, not just man and woman, but mankind."[35] This play brought O'Neill a third Pulitzer Prize and enjoyed a long Broadway run of 426 performances.

O'Neill earned more than \$275,000 from *Strange Interlude* in the 1920s, a sizable amount at the time.[36] He was finally able to live a prosperous lifestyle based solely on his writing.

O'Neill Brings Modernism to Studies of Good and Evil *Dynamo*, *Mourning Becomes Electra*, and *Days Without End*

> *"I have not had any idea of living over here permanently. No nonsense such as renouncing America. There's such a thing as being sensibly patriotic. But living away from America has been a good way to know how to see things that you couldn't see before."*
>
> —Eugene O'Neill on his 1928–31 residence in France[1]

Immediately after *Strange Interlude*'s success in 1928, Eugene O'Neill, separated from his wife Agnes, traveled abroad with Carlotta Monterey. Carlotta had about as much money as O'Neill, was rather a snob, and liked to live in high style. Although the couple agreed to contribute equally to their expenses, they did not always agree on what to buy.

They proceeded to rent a lavish French villa far outside Paris, so O'Neill could work undisturbed on the draft of his next play, *Dynamo*. Usually when absorbed in his writing, O'Neill drank less. But getting used to life with Carlotta in a foreign country proved taxing. Both were temperamental people. With Agnes balking at the divorce terms, O'Neill

O'Neill sits with his third wife, Carlotta, in 1931. The two first met when she starred in his play *The Hairy Ape*.

got drunk from the stress, causing blowups with Carlotta. Somehow Carlotta did not realize the level of risk life could be with O'Neill, saying "Why drink, when you know you are not sane with alcohol in you? Literally not sane . . . it's dangerous!"[2]

O'Neill forged ahead with *Dynamo,* feeling under pressure to produce another hit play. The result was writing that slid to a substandard level. O'Neill sent *Dynamo* off to the Theatre Guild at the end of August 1928 without doing his usual thorough revision. Given the success of *Strange Interlude,* the Guild quickly optioned this play and put it into production. O'Neill knew the play had many problems—but he would not leave Europe and Carlotta to go to New York to fix them.

Dynamo: O'Neill Explores Conflicts of Religion vs. Science

Dynamo opened in New York on February 11, 1929, to harsh reviews, and played less than two months to Theatre Guild subscribers. The play's theme, the relationship between electricity and the life force itself, was modern in concept, yet as dated as Mary Shelley's 1818 novel *Frankenstein.* By the end of the 1920s, hydroelectric plants hummed across the land, making electricity generally accessible. Yet O'Neill knew many people were baffled by its nearly incomprehensible power. Electricity signified to O'Neill the new, godlike power of science itself.

O'Neill creates two families in *Dynamo,* the Lights and the Fifes, who are neighbors and yet antagonists. Reverend Hutchins Light, a fanatic Christian preacher, teaches his teenage son Reuben to fear lightning as a symbol of God's retribution, and to beware the anti-religious attitudes of scientists. Ramsay Fife, an equally opinionated man, is the superintendent of the town's hydroelectric plant. He is pleased that his daughter Ada is an independent, modern young girl who accepts his atheism. In the course of the play, Ada comes to believe profoundly in the love she feels for Reuben. As Reuben travels and matures, his adoration of the power of electricity absorbs him. His new religious icon is the dynamo. O'Neill describes it as having "something of a massive female idol about it."[3]

In *Dynamo* all six characters mutter out loud to themselves at unexpected moments. Unlike in *Strange Interlude*, where spoken asides were skillfully handled to suggest the hidden urges of the subconscious, the people in *Dynamo* blurt out their mundane observations for no apparent purpose. May Fife, the dull mother of Ada, announces sleepily to no one: "The sun is hot . . . I feel so dozy . . . I know why dogs love to lie in the sun . . . and cats and chickens . . . they forget to think they're living."[4]

The play's most developed character is young Reuben Light, who turns into a fanatic follower of what he believes is the new religion of science. He tells Ada that she must believe in the Dynamo-Mother Electricity: "her song is the hymn of eternal generation, the song of eternal life!"[5] When O'Neill writes his tragic finale in which Reuben purifies the urges of his unworthy flesh by shooting Ada and throwing himself on the dynamo to be electrocuted, we are not certain what the point is of his sacrifice. For this misguided young hero, we see no promise of eternal life.

Dynamo poses many questions. Is the source of all life and rebirth found in electric power? Are all gods—from the Greek pantheon through Jehovah, Christ, Mohammed, down to mysterious power embodied in electricity—able either to save or destroy mankind? Does religion involve only the mind and spirit, and force the believer to vilify the flesh? Is the twentieth

The action on stage revolves around a huge power plant in this production of *Dynamo*.

century an age in which man must question whether God is dead?

O'Neill claimed he wrote the play in haste ("It had the makings of a fine play, but I did it too fast"). Yet it is hard to believe that even with revisions, O'Neill could have salvaged this confusing piece. George Jean Nathan summed up the critical attitude in his March 1929 article in *American Mercury*: "When O'Neill feels, he often produces something that is very beautiful, very moving and very fine. But when he gives himself over to science and philosophy, as in *Dynamo*, he would seem to be lost."[6]

Mourning Becomes Electra: An Ancient Plot Moves to America

O'Neill would work his way back to the top of his form as the premier author of tragedy when he conceived of an American version of the *Oresteia*. In order to concentrate on this masterpiece, he needed to straighten out of his personal life. On July 2, 1929, he finally received his divorce from Agnes. Knowing he'd not been a great husband to her, he granted Agnes generous alimony and child support. She in return granted him open visitation with their children.

O'Neill married Carlotta Monterey in Paris on July 21. They continued their life together at the château outside Tours, France, where Carlotta directed some remodeling, and installed a large swimming pool so Eugene could enjoy his daily exercise. He purchased a Bugatti sports car which he drove speedily around the back roads. Eugene Jr., then a Yale graduate, made a successful visit and seemed to get on with Carlotta. Many New York theatre friends also vacationed there with the newlyweds.

In order to tackle his new, demanding play, it appears that O'Neill tried to repress his alcoholism. He had stayed dry from 1926–1928, then had lapses on and off. Carlotta kept cases of Coca-Cola handy for such times.

When writing *Mourning Becomes Electra*, O'Neill wrote to a friend on August 28, 1930, about his use of the plot of the *Oresteia*: "I modernize this story to a psychological drama of human interrelationships, using no Gods or heroes. . . . Don't get the idea there is a lot of Greek stuff in this. I simply pinch their plot, as many a better playwright has done before me, and make of it a modern psychological drama."[7] His setting of the story in an America torn by civil war, where only the old, powerful New England families survived financially, shows he is doing more than merely writing a psychological family drama. He is taking an entire society to task.

The Mannon family represents the nineteenth-century version of the House of Atreus. The play is set in the Mannons' Greek-revival-style mansion in a New England seaport community in 1865–1866. Christine Mannon describes the house as being like "a sepulcher! The 'whited' one of the Bible—pagan temple front stuck like a mask on Puritan gray ugliness!"[8] Classical Greek imagery melds with the Puritan social ethic.

The American Civil War years of 1865–66 replaces the Trojan War experience. The Menelaus-Helen-Paris story line is deleted. Although the character and sacrifice of Iphigeneia is also expunged, the Electra-Orestes story remains. Lavinia Mannon replaces Electra, and her brother Orin stands in for Orestes. The Clytemnestra-Aegisthus affair is still a trigger, now replaced by Christine Mannon and her secret sexual relationship with sea captain Adam Brant. Agamemnon's reincarnation is General Ezra Mannon, a judge and a ship

O'NEILL RECREATES THE TRAGEDIES OF AESCHYLUS'S *ORESTEIA*

In Aeschylus's *Oresteia*, the House of Atreus dwells in the Kingdom of Argos in Greece. Atreus is father to Agamemnon and Menelaus. These men inherit Atreus's kingdom. Agamemnon weds Clytemnestra of Sparta and fathers daughters Iphigeneia and Electra, and son Orestes. Menelaus weds Helen of Sparta, who is seduced by Paris of Troy. Agamemnon and Menelaus prepare for war on Troy. Agamemnon slays his daughter Iphigeneia in sacrifice to the goddess Diana before his army departs. Troy is defeated and its people enslaved.

After the defeat of Troy, Agamemnon takes Trojan sorceress Cassandra as his mistress. His wife Clytemnestra then takes Aegisthus as her lover. When her son Orestes protests, she banishes him. After Agamemnon returns home with Cassandra, Clytemnestra kills him and his mistress. Electra, devoted to her father, vows to avenge him. Bonded with Orestes, they carry out a plot to kill their mother, Clytemnestra, and her lover Aegisthus. The Furies, spirits of retribution, drive Orestes out of Argos. This leaves Electra alone to mourn her family.

company owner, as well as an officer in the Union Army. O'Neill set the play in the nineteenth century, when a slightly more formal way of speaking was common. This gave a heightened sense of classic drama while still being essentially American.

O'Neill formally divided this work into three parts: "Homecoming—A Play in Four Acts," "The Hunted—A Play in Five Acts," and "The Haunted—A Play in Four Acts."

In the first play, "Homecoming," we meet a group of humble townspeople celebrating the surrender of the Confederacy, while showing their suspicions of the upper-crust Mannons. Among them is Seth, the family's old groundskeeper and confidant, a source of exposition about the Mannon family history.

Lavinia Mannon, the thin, rigid, and determined twenty-three-year-old daughter, seems more masculine than her brother Orin. We learn she has gone to New York, for private reasons that old Seth seems to comprehend. We soon realize that Lavinia is distrustful and spies on her mother, Christine. Her mother claims that Lavinia is unnatural, and has always tried to become "the wife of your father and the mother of Orin! You've always schemed to steal my place!"[9] Lavinia will evolve throughout the trilogy into her father's avenger, her brother's motivator, and the agent of her mother's destruction. Her suitor Peter Niles is crushed when Lavinia bursts out: "I don't know anything about love! I don't want to know anything! I hate love!"[10] Her almost abnormal attachment to her father is growing; she explodes when her father is murdered. Peter Niles cannot comprehend the nature of Lavinia's passion for her father.

Christine Mannon, Ezra Mannon's attractive, sensuous forty-year-old wife, is Lavinia and Orin's mother. Her frequent

Performers act out a scene from the *Oresteia* by Aeschylus, an ancient Greek play that is retold in *Mourning Becomes Electra*.

visits to New York to check on her ailing doctor-father are cover-ups for a chance to rendezvous with Adam Brant, her younger, sea captain lover. Her relationship with the older, sober Ezra was strained long ago, and now her love for Adam keeps her vital. Her main concern, besides concealing her adultery, is keeping her beauty. She says: "I'm afraid of time."[11] Christine's deepest ties have always been to her son.

Adam Brant, a dashing sea captain, has his own issues with the Mannon family. By becoming Christine Mannon's lover, he gets back at them. Seth reveals that the name "Brant" comes from Marie Brancome, a young Canadian girl who was a nursemaid to the sister of Lavinia's grandfather, Abe Mannon. When Abe's brother David Mannon got her pregnant, she bore his son Adam. This makes Adam a cousin to Ezra Mannon. When Marie needed money to survive, the Mannons ignored her and let her die, embittering her son against them. Adam tells Lavinia: "I swore on my mother's body I'd [avenge] her death on him."[12]

Ezra Mannon, Lavinia and Orin's father, age fifty, returns from the war weary and obsessed with death. He senses his wife Christine is "more beautiful than ever—and strange to me. I don't know you. You're younger."[13] He does not guess the reason for her new bloom. Surviving war's battles has freed him to think about life. He observes that the Mannons thought "life was a dying. Being born was starting to die . . . how in hell people ever got such notions!"[14] He then appeals to Christine to explain why they grew distant. "I loved you then," he says, "and all the years between, and I love you now."[15] Yet he cannot get his wife's passion for him to rekindle.

Orin Mannon, Lavinia's brother, about twenty-one, returns at the start of the second play, "The Hunted." Worn and depressed from battle, he tells his sister: "My mind is still full of ghosts. I can't grasp anything but war. . . . Vinnie, give me a chance to get used to things!"[16] His emotional health is fragile, which makes him easy for his sister to manipulate in her scheme of revenge.

In the third act of "Homecoming," set in April 1865, we see that Lavinia, having detected her mother's affair, wants to tell her father Ezra on his return home. Ezra goes to bed with Christine before Lavinia has a chance. After their night together, Ezra senses that his home is not his own. He knows the house—and his wife—are waiting for another. Christine confesses that she has never been truly his. "Homecoming" ends as Ezra, suffering from angina, begs for his medication. Christine gives him poison instead. Lavinia, learning in a dream that her father needs her, rushes in to hear his accusation: "She's guilty—not medicine."[17] When Ezra dies, Lavinia swears she will make her mother pay for her crime and keep her away from Adam.

In act one of "The Hunted," we hear from people exiting the mansion that Christine appears to be a wreck over Ezra's death. Lavinia is cold as an icicle and will not display her grief. Christine tells Hazel Niles, who loves her son Orin, that God will not leave people alone: "[H]e twists and wrings and tortures our lives with others' lives until—we poison each other to death!"[18] When Orin arrives for his father's funeral, we see he is deeply affected by his battle experiences. After observing his mother, Christine, having a rendezvous with her lover, Adam, Orin shoots him in a rage. Lavinia speaks to Adam's corpse: "How could you love that vile old woman so? But you're dead! May God find forgiveness for your sins. May the soul of our cousin, Adam Mannon, rest in peace."[19] Orin replies: "Rest in hell, you mean!" and then observes, "By God, he does look like Father." Orin has killed his father-image, and hopes to regain his mother's primary love—a classic Greek tragic theme. Christine, in despair, commits suicide. Orin's mental state begins to crumble from guilt and grief.

In "The Haunted," the third play, Lavinia has sailed with Orin on a yearlong voyage to the Far East and South Pacific. She has blossomed, taking on her mother's looks and feminine confidence. Orin experiences morbid spells and accuses Lavinia of stealing his mother's soul. A month later, Orin talks to his father's portrait while writing a confession of his murder of Adam Brant and why. Lavinia is terrified Orin will implicate her. Evil spirits, guilty consciences, ghosts of the victims, haunt Lavinia and Orin. Lavinia realizes Orin is going mad—but cannot stop him from taking his life. Declaring she is through with the Mannons forever, she says: "I'm Mother's daughter—not one of you! I'll live in spite of you!"[20] Like the cursed mortals who once offended the Greek gods, Lavinia finds she cannot escape the dead and their secrets. As she retreats into the house, she says: "It takes the Mannons to punish themselves for being born."[21] Critics have called this the least symbolic of O'Neill's major plays—it is a real tale of crime and punishment by clearly drawn characters who move toward their convincing destiny.

Mourning Becomes Electra rehearsed a full seven weeks, instead of the usual four. The ever-present O'Neill kept trimming and altering the lines. Although the play ran an hour longer than the lengthy *Strange Interlude*, the producers decided to present the show in one day.

The Broadway critics of 1931 viewed the six-hour performance in a state of ecstasy. In one extremely long sentence, critic John Mason Brown from the *New York Evening Post* praised the play: "For exciting proof that the theatre is still very much alive, that it still has grandeur and ecstasy to offer to its patrons, that fine acting has not disappeared from behind the footlights' glare, that productions that thrill with memorability are still being made, that scenic design and stage direction can belong among the fine arts, . . . you have only to journey to the Guild Theatre these nights and days and sit before Eugene O'Neill's new trilogy '*Mourning Becomes Electra*.'"[22]

Days Without End: O'Neill Asks, Can Religion Bring Redemption?

Resuming an exploration of his youthful religious education and crisis of faith that drove him from the Catholic Church, Eugene O'Neill expanded a scenario he had written in 1927. He called it *Days Without End*, hoping it would expand on themes of human frailty, guilt, doubt, faith, and redemption that he tried to work in *Dynamo*. This play also tried to cover too many areas of contemporary life and religion to make a satisfactory artistic statement.

John Loving is a New York businessman, suffering due to the economic depression of 1932. He and his partner William Eliot are barely staying in business, yet they keep up the office. John fills his spare time by working on a novel, which secretly reflects his inner life.

Loving is John's alternate personality, a doppelgänger, or hidden inner demon that speaks to John, deriding his beliefs, goals, and faith. This role is played by a second actor. Loving wears a "death mask of a John who has died with a sneer of scornful mockery on his lips."[23] Loving can be heard by the audience and John, and seemingly by John's uncle, the kindly Father Matthew Baird, a Catholic priest. Father Baird's role is to try to bring John back to the church.

Lucy Hillman, wife of John and William's friend Walter, is abused by her unfaithful, drunkard husband. A friend of

John's wife, she was briefly John's lover during a time when her husband said they should try having affairs.

Elsa Loving, John's wife, had an earlier unhappy marriage. Through faith and her relationship with her second husband John, Elsa is fulfilled. She loves John more than ever, because she tells Lucy "he's become my child and father now, as well as being a husband."[24] When Lucy tells Elsa about having an affair, and Elsa thinks about the details in John's writing, she realizes it was John that was Lucy's lover. Furious, she sneers at him: "So it was you who told on yourself . . . Rather a joke on you, isn't it?"[25] When the wife in John's novel dies, Elsa feels he imagines this fate for herself.

This play also explores hidden and conflicting aspects of the characters' psychologies, as O'Neill did in *The Great God Brown* and *Strange Interlude*. It resolves into a piece centered on John, who—perhaps representing an aspect of O'Neill himself—is placed in the role of an earthly pilgrim. The Devil's Advocate (Loving) and the Voice of God (Father Baird) pull him back and forth. No other characters receive much development, although Elsa seems fairly believable.

John's quest is to regain faith in redemption and eternal life. At the end of his "novel" his wife dies and the hero never returns to the Church. When Elsa runs out into chilling rain, still weakened from the flu, John realizes she believes her death, like the wife in his novel, is the will of God—or fate. As Elsa languishes from pneumonia, Dr. Stillwell tells Father Baird she is refusing to fight for her life. When the priest gets John to pray for Elsa's survival, John says: "Let Him prove to me His Love exists! Then I will believe in Him again."[26] Father Baird orders John not to bargain with God. Arguing against his inner fear and doubt, John recalls that he once cursed God when his parents were taken from him. As John runs away in despair, Elsa awakes and forgives him.

The finale set in John's boyhood church features a life-size crucifix. John and Loving debate until Loving's unbelief is crushed. When Father Baird tells him that Elsa will live and still loves him, John cries "I know! Love lives forever. Death is dead! Life laughs with God's love again. Life laughs with love."[27]

When the Theatre Guild produced the play in 1934, audiences could not get absorbed in O'Neill's soul-searching. Major critics like Brooks Atkinson at the *New York Times* commented that *Days Without End* was "written as if O'Neill had never written a play before."[28] Critic Bernard Sobel at the *New York Daily Mirror* nailed it by saying "*Days Without End* is almost as laborious as its title implies."[29] Some critics appreciated the poetry and search for the meaning of man's relationship with God, and religious-based publications praised it. However, the work was so ultimately embarrassing for Eugene O'Neill that he gave up the notion of *Dynamo* and *Days Without End* being a modernist trilogy. He moved on to greater works with nostalgic settings and new themes.

---

modernism

The belief that a play need not be staged in exactly the same style, language, and dialect as originally written by the author.

"Those Dear Old Days!": O'Neill Takes a Look From the Past in *Ah, Wilderness!*, *The Iceman Cometh*, and *A Touch of the Poet*

In the 1930s Eugene O'Neill could have rested on his laurels. He had written enough great plays to live off their royalties and reputations. Instead of winding down, he became even more ambitious, thinking in terms of "cycles" of plays—cycles as large as nine at a time. He had always written by hand using a pencil. Dictating to a secretary never worked well for him. So in order to keep up production on all these planned dramas, O'Neill needed his physical strength, something that was beginning to fail.

During this period, O'Neill suffered from gastritis, prostate problems, and a nearly burst appendix. He still smoked constantly. His liver showed amazingly little damage due to alcoholism, but he began to have symptoms of nervous tremors. The O'Neills, like almost every other American family with wealth, also took a hit from the Great Depression. They had bought too much real estate, and O'Neill's publisher,

O'Neill works in his library around 1932. The playwright always insisted on writing out his plays in longhand, a practice which became more difficult as his health deteriorated.

Horace Liveright, was almost bankrupt. For once, O'Neill had a real reason for feeling depressed.

In March 1934, after *Days Without End* flopped, O'Neill went for an exam by his New York physician. This doctor said his weight was dangerously low (around 140 pounds) and he would have a complete collapse if he did not eat better and rest. At this time insulin injections were used to increase appetite, but they had side effects of headaches and nervousness, as well as shakiness in the hands. O'Neill's depression worsened, until he was able to work again.

What O'Neill's doctors could not know at this time was that his cerebellar vermis (the brain center that coordinates muscle movement) was starting to lose necessary cells.[1] This brain decline continued, causing the tremors that nearly ruined his writing and physical control. The condition appeared at the time to be a form of Parkinson's Disease. The true source of this condition was not determined until an autopsy revealed it after O'Neill's death.

O'Neill wrote *Ah, Wilderness!* in 1932–1933, *A Touch of the Poet* in 1938–1939, and *The Iceman Cometh* in 1937–1939. These three plays written in the 1930s helped audiences retreat to different times, far from the present concerns of the economic Depression and the threat of war in Europe. Nostalgia was what audiences craved. O'Neill set *Ah, Wilderness!* in a 1906 New London, Connecticut, home, plus a nearby bar and beach. *The Iceman Cometh* takes place in a 1912 New York City saloon. *A Touch of the Poet* occurs in an 1828 tavern outside Boston. Each play touches somewhat on O'Neill's early dedication to left-wing politics and socialism. But politics are used more to illuminate the characters and their problems than to promote the liberal agenda.

The structures and styles of these works show O'Neill's range. *Ah, Wilderness!* uses the format of romantic comedy, featuring a teenage boy experiencing the "wilderness" of youth, living in his world of poetry, and enduring angst over his love for innocent Muriel. The tone of this play is warm, sometimes humorous, as it recreates old New London and its fictional newspaper editor and his family. O'Neill may have regarded the Miller family as the one he always wanted for himself. He claimed he wrote the scenario in twenty-four hours in September 1932 and completed the play in less than six weeks.[2] *Ah, Wilderness!* portrays the affectionate interdependence of the Millers, who deal gently but firmly with the problems of the children's maturation. Darker issues of sexual repression and immorality, alcoholism, and loneliness are certainly part of the Miller family's world. But they are handled in the context of the concerned, supportive family unit.

The Iceman Cometh is a naturalistic drama, which places archetypal characters in their natural habitat, Harry Hope's Saloon, to explore the effects of dreams and denial. Members of this sorry group are linked in their own special interdependence. O'Neill describes the saloon as "a cheap ginmill of the five-cent whiskey, last-resort variety situated on the downtown West Side of New York."[3] During his early days as a destitute writer and drunk, O'Neill virtually lived in such places and met a crew of has-beens who kept each other going with mutual self-pity. The play was set in 1912, a low year personally for O'Neill, the one in which he attempted suicide. He told George Jean Nathan that the play's locale was a "composite of three places" where he used to drink with the men who inspired these characters.[4]

Surrounded by Harry Hope, his two pimp bartenders, and a trio of stalwart prostitutes, ten ragged characters spend time in an alcoholic haze, subsisting on pipe dreams. They all await Theodore Hickman, a hearty hardware salesman who feeds their self-delusions and their drinking habits on his regular visits. This time, Harry's residents are shocked by "Hickey" and his new philosophy of blasting open one's dreams. The play becomes a conflict between the group and Hickey, until one side must destroy the other. In the end, no one achieves the goal of stopping time and resuming past roles. The tragedy is that Hickey preached it was futile for them to even try—that true peace is achieved when all illusions are finally destroyed.

> **socialism**
>
> A school of political thought that includes any philosophy that advocates collective ownership of property and group control of the production and distribution of goods.

A Touch of the Poet, while taking the format of a family melodrama, explored some of *The Iceman Cometh*'s themes. Always fascinated with Irish immigrants and their ability to thrive or fail in Yankee New England, O'Neill created the memorable Melody family. With his unfailing ear for taking Irish brogue and blending it with early American slang, O'Neill wrote the roles of Cornelius and Nora Melody. This 19th century Irish-born couple now live outside Boston and dream of becoming middle-class. Their daughter Sara speaks proper American, but can assume an Irish brogue to goad her father.

The theme shared by both *The Iceman* and *Poet* is that of self-delusion and dreams being necessary to the poets of the world to sustain their life. Another theme is that of using alcohol to fuel courage and retain one's pride. However, the finale of *Poet* finds the self-absorbed poseur Cornelius forced to face the true image of himself—and go on with his life. His dependent wife, Nora, and daughter, Sara, almost sad to see Cornelius stop his pretenses and become his simple, lower-class self, are also relieved that their lives will now probably improve.

Ah, Wilderness!: O'Neill Inhabits His Dream Family

O'Neill told his friend Lawrence Langner that he wrote *Ah, Wilderness!* as a "gesture toward a more comprehensive, unembittered understanding and inner freedom."[5] O'Neill revisited his boyhood home, Monte Cristo Cottage, in 1931 and recalled both the good and bad times his family had experienced spending their summers there. The rooms he described for Nat Miller's home are based on the O'Neills' cottage on Pequot Avenue. The seaside locale is Ocean Beach in New London. Richard Miller's beloved Muriel is a homage to O'Neill's girl-friend Maibelle Scott, as well as other Connecticut belles. The understanding O'Neill is drawing upon came from the first summer when his family was relatively happy, and young Eugene was researching the meaning of life and love.

We meet the Miller family (actually a blend of the New London families of postmaster John McGinley and newspaper editor Fred Latimer) as they spend a Fourth (and Fifth) of July together. Nat Miller, in his fifties, needs all the wisdom he can muster to keep his family members on track and his community newspaper selling. Essie Miller is still sweetly attractive at age fifty. Her managerial abilities to run a large family are a big part of her identity. Along with the four children we meet in the play, she has two older sons, plus a sister-in-law and brother who need her affection and guidance. Arthur Miller, an athletic nineteen-year-old Yale student, is admired by his younger siblings. His attempts at sophistication include pipe smoking and dating lovely women.

Richard Miller, the seventeen-year-old "hero" on the threshold of leaving home for college, is the family concern. His father says, "Poetry's his meat nowadays—love poetry— and socialism too, I suspect from some dire declarations he's made."[6] Too old to be disciplined, too young to be trusted in saloons, Richard is a handful. Mildred Miller, bright and trim at age fifteen, loves to tease her brothers. Tommy Miller, an eleven-year-old energetic boy, completes the family and gives his mother fits. Lily Miller, Nat's sister, is a forty-two-year-old unmarried schoolteacher, shy but very kind. Sid Davis, Essie's brother, is past fifty-five, a troubled jokester with a drinking problem, although he manages to hold onto Lily's affections.

These characters have spent their lives together and know each other's strengths and failings well. In trying to cope with Richard's coming-of-age dilemmas, they unite to guide him and ready him for his future as a young adult. Sid's alcoholism is a darker, long-term problem that the family must absorb without solving.

The two most touching scenes in *Ah, Wilderness!* involve Richard trying to achieve manhood and relate to women. Act Three opens with Richard taking refuge in a hotel bar with Belle, one of O'Neill's more unappealing prostitutes. Richard has been brought here by Wint, an older friend who has taken another prostitute upstairs. After struggling with alcohol, guilt, and the image of Muriel, Richard finds he cannot take Belle to bed—but ends up giving her a kiss, a drink, and a poetry recitation!

Act Four begins with Richard's sister Mildred delivering a secret letter from Muriel, to Richard's delight: "She says she didn't mean a word in that other letter. Her old man made her write it. And she loves me and only me and always will, no matter how they punish her!"[7] When Mildred indicates she is surprised at Muriel's spunk, Richard states: "Think I could fall in love with a girl that was afraid to say her soul's her own?"[8] When Richard waits for Muriel secretly on the beach, his interior monologue reflects all the insecurity of the young romantic. Forgetting his cynicism, he exclaims that the night

A scene from the 1935 MGM film *Ah, Wilderness!* (left to right: Frank Albertson, Eric Linden, and Cecilia Parker).

was made for him and Muriel: "Gee, I love tonight. I love the sand and the trees, and the grass, and the water and the sky and the moon . . . it's all in me and I'm in it. God, it's so beautiful!"[9] Richard's decency is rewarded, as Muriel pledges him her love.

A final moment of depth and honesty between father Nat and son Richard help audiences believe in the future of the American family. The play resolves itself as sweetly as a fragrant summer night, with the long-married Nat and Essie dimming the lights, kissing each other, and heading for bed.

O'Neill wrote to his friend George Jean Nathan nostalgically about this play: "Ah Wilderness, those dear old days were you and I were little convent boys together . . . Life was so simple then."[10] The audiences and critics must have felt the same affection, because *Ah, Wilderness!* played to more theatergoers in New York than any other O'Neill play during his lifetime, except for *Strange Interlude*.

O'NEILL'S MAJOR AWARDS

O'Neill's plays took the Pulitzer Prize for drama a record four times: *Beyond the Horizon* in 1920, *Anna Christie* in 1922, *Strange Interlude* in 1928, and (posthumously) *Long Day's Journey Into Night* in 1956. On November 12, 1936, O'Neill was to be awarded the highest international honor: the Nobel Prize for Literature. Although physically unable to fly to Stockholm to accept, he sent a speech to be read, where he gave credit to Swedish playwright August Strindberg as a strong influence on his work. His award read: "To Eugene O'Neill for the power, honesty, and deep-felt emotions of his dramatic works, which embody an original concept of tragedy."[11]

The Iceman Cometh: Seventeen Sorry Souls Plus a Ghost

While working on *The Iceman Cometh* in 1937, Eugene O'Neill and his wife, Carlotta, moved into a house they built in Danville, California. As he was attempting to create a large cycle of plays, he worried that the world was darkening. During 1938 and 1939, the Nazi government of Germany was invading Austria, the Sudetenland, Czechoslovakia, and Poland. The specter of war affected O'Neill's state of mind. He indicated in letters: "in these times . . . nothing seems of less importance than whether another play is produced or not produced."[12]

O'Neill's physical problems worsened, reducing his ability to work. The prospect of the strain of rehearsal and production in New York so overwhelmed him that O'Neill completed *The Iceman Cometh*, then did not submit it for production. He told George Jean Nathan that he did like the play, especially the title, "which I love, because it characteristically expresses so much of the outer and the inner spirit of the play."[13] He stated that he tried to write the dialogue in "exact lingo of place and 1912 as I remember it."[14] O'Neill believed the play hit as deeply and truly into the farce and humor, pity, and ironic tragedy of life as anything written in modern drama.

Who were the inhabitants of Harry Hope's saloon? Harry Hope, the proprietor, and his brother-in-law Ed Mosher, a one-time circus manager, both sixty, are tired, lonely Irishmen. Pat McGloin, an ousted policeman, and Joe Mott, an angry black man who lost his gambling house, are about fifty and tend to be adversaries. Old-time enemies are three men once involved in the Boer War: Piet Wejoen, a Boer commando; James "Jimmy Tomorrow" Cameron, a Boer War correspon-

O'Neill enjoys the beach with his wife, Carlotta, around 1938.

dent; and Cecil Lewis, a British Infantry captain who fought the Boers. Two men who once led the Anarchist movement, Hugo Kalmar and Larry Slade, in their fifties, are lost souls without a cause. Two younger men are thrown into the mix: Willie Oban, late thirties, who graduated Harvard Law School but failed to become an attorney due to alcoholism, and Don Parritt, eighteen, whose mother is a jailed leader from the Anarchist movement. Parritt tries to get Slade's attention and compassion, but Slade loved Parritt's mother and decides the boy sold her out. Also important in this panorama of desperate dreamers are the tough Italian bartenders, Rocky and Chuck. Rocky pimps out the young prostitutes Pearl, Margie, and Cora—but Cora is determined to marry Chuck. Into the saloon comes Theodore "Hickey" Hickman, age fifty. As a traveling salesman, he is a classic character on the American landscape. Hickey tries to bring the group a kind of peace through the annihilation of their dreams.

The Anarchist Larry Slade left the Movement years ago because, he says, "men didn't want to be saved from themselves, for that would mean they'd have to give up greed, and they'll never pay that price for liberty."[15] However, Larry waits for Hickey, because he is "a great one to make a joke of everything and cheer you up."[16] Rocky the bartender recalls how Hickey, when very drunk, tells a tale about weeping for his wife—and then suddenly announces that she is fine, he left her in bed with the iceman. Since in 1912 the iceman delivered daily blocks to the kitchens of every American housewife, the story took on a universal reality. The men at Harry's assume Hickey was joking, since the iceman really seducing Mrs. Hickey would not be amusing. The term "iceman" was also period slang for the undertaker, as corpses were put on ice until they could be prepared for burial. Carried one step further, the iceman would be a term for Death. In a way, Mrs. Hickey becomes the seventeenth character—although perhaps a ghostly one—in the play.

Joe Mott, the black gambler, has his own take on the Anarchists and the Socialist Movement. He says the Anarchist is just a freeloader; but the Socialist often has a job and "he's bound by his religion to split fifty-fifty with you . . . So you don't shoot no Socialists while I'm around."[17] Larry Slade has to admit that Joe has both the truth of human nature and the practical wisdom of the world figured out.

Don Parritt finds himself in what Larry calls the No Chance Saloon, the End of the Line Café, seeking solace after his Anarchist mother was arrested for a bombing. He resented his mother's neglect of him—but cannot believe in her cause, which he terms a crazy pipe dream. McGloin and Mosher hide from the reality of their pasts: Hope terms them "an old grafting flatfoot and a circus bunco steerer!"[18] Hope's pipe dream is that he was about to be nominated for alderman, but lost heart for public service when his wife died. About to celebrate his sixtieth birthday, Hope tells himself it is not too late. The Brit and the Boer embrace the dream of returning to their homelands as soon as some mythical estate is settled, but have turned their lives into one long drunken wait.

The arrival of Hickey changes the tone and direction of the plot. Announcing that all will be grateful when he shows them that their liquor-laden world of delusion is wrong, Hickey claims that all will learn through tough truth: "You'll know what real peace means . . . because you won't be scared of either life or death any more. You simply won't give a damn! Any more than I do."[19]

The play becomes an examination of truth versus pipe dreams, truth being relative to the viewpoint of the teller.

Hickey becomes the harsh light in everyone's eyes and the thorn in their sides, until they long to get rid of him. Gradually, through Act Four, Hickey destroys every illusion left in the saloon, then goes to work on his own reality. Eventually Hickey gives himself up to the police after claiming that he shot his wife to give her peace. "Do you suppose I give a damn about life now?" he asks the police officer. "Why you bonehead, I haven't got a single damned lying hope or pipe dream left!"[20]

Harry Hope and his fellow barflies agree they will testify that Hickey was crazy, hoping this will keep him out of the electric chair. Now they can return to their pipe dream at the bottom of a bottle, allowing them to exist until the iceman (death) truly comes.

In this play, says critic John Patrick Diggins, "The desperate derelicts wait for Hickey, the messiah who turns out to be a murderer. O'Neill also waits, even while knowing there will be no arrival, no deliverance from the human condition. Can life have a purpose if it must end in death?"[21] For O'Neill, this will always be the balancing act.

A Touch of the Poet: More Pipe Dreamers Battle Reality

The crowd of middle-aged Irish immigrants that opens the play in the Melody Tavern taproom make one wonder if Eugene O'Neill ever knew a sober Irishman. These good-natured cronies—Mickey Maloy, Jamie Cregan, and later on, Dan Roche, Paddy O'Down, and Patch Riley—deliver all the prehistory and psychological background needed to understand proprietor Cornelius Melody and his family. Once Nora Melody enters, bowed down from hard labor but with an inner glow of lifelong love for Cornelius, we see the true strength of the Irish race: the wife and mother. The American daughter, Sara, longing to wed a Yankee heir recuperating in the tavern's rented room, shows a tough determination to succeed in nineteenth-century America.

The play's central figure, however, is Cornelius Melody, called "Con" by his family. Once a major in the British armed forces and son of an Irish landowner, Con Melody has seen his pipe dreams of making a fortune in America evaporate. O'Neill calls him "a Byronic hero, noble, embittered, disdainful, defying his tragic fate, brooding over past glories."[22] Although Con is a pretentious man who treats his wife and daughter like slaves, his grandeur and style left over from his early life afford him a fascination. A secondary character, Deborah Harford, is the mother of Sara's unseen lover, Simon Harford. Her visit to the Melody Tavern to investigate the girl her son loves begins as a disaster when Cornelius stupidly makes a pass at her—but ends positively as she approves of the strong Sara. The other secondary player is Nicholas Gadsby, Henry Harford's attorney, who arrives to buy the Melody family off with a handsome offer to relocate to Ohio. Con and his pals throw him out. Two influential but unseen characters are Simon Harford, the man Sara is nursing and wishes to marry, and, believe it or not, Cornelius's horse! This thoroughbred mare that he adores is the living vestige of his former military and social stature in Ireland.

The concept of love being a powerful factor in life carries through *A Touch of the Poet*. For Nora Melody, husband Con's love has been the cornerstone of her otherwise drab existence. For Cornelius Melody, the peasant Nora, whom he had to marry due to her pregnancy, is regarded as a millstone around his neck, yet he cannot help caring for her. These characters hark back to Robert and Ruth Mayo in O'Neill's first major play, *Beyond the Horizon*. Robert Mayo, a member of a farming family, gives up his dream of being a roaming writer to wed Ruth. When Robert is introduced in the stage directions, O'Neill writes "There is a touch of the poet about him."[23] Marrying Ruth does indeed set Robert on a tragic path, as he transfers his love from Ruth to his daughter.

Love becomes a reality in Sara Melody's heart. Sara realizes that she not only wants Simon Harford to take her away from her miserable role as her father's tavern waitress, but that she truly cares for the boy. Sadly, Sara fears that loving Simon may be a tragic trap: "I'm too much in love and I don't want to be!" she tells her mother. "I won't let my heart rule my head and make a slave of me!"[24] Yet her mother assures her at the end that her marriage to a once-fine man trapped by pride and delusion has been worth it: "I'll play any game he likes and give him love in it. Haven't I always? Sure, I have no pride at all—except that."

Prideful love for his beautiful white horse, a symbol of his former military importance, must end for Cornelius. He shoots the mare with "the Major's" dueling pistols. This forces him to kill "the Major" as well, and assume the role of modest immigrant tavern keeper he truly is. Some critics noticed a parallel between *The Iceman* and *Poet*. Jordan Miller said: "The 'practical' Melody . . . is an empty man, just as the inhabitants of Harry Hope's bar are hollow men revealed for what they truly are when they face up to reality."[25]

In a way, Cornelius's decline makes Nora's life easier—Con might actually help her do the work of running the business— and it forces Con to join the world of his cronies. Con says of his murdering his mare: "she saw I was dying with her. She understood! She forgave me!"[26] About the Major: "he won't haunt me for long . . . I intend to live at my ease from now on

O'Neill, seated, discusses *The Iceman Cometh* with actors during a rehearsal in 1946 (left to right: Ruth Gilbert, Dudley Digges, and Marcella Markham).

and not let the dead bother me."[27] Con will bury his uniform and "bloody England," and let his daughter be the one to achieve social success.

Broadway Productions

A Touch of the Poet was planned as a part of a cycle of plays, the theme of which was the immigrant's role in America, where greed and lust for power prevailed over idealism. O'Neill drafted the next play, *More Stately Mansions*, in which Sara Melody becomes the driving character. Writing cycles of plays, however, was too great an effort for O'Neill physically and emotionally. Both *The Iceman Cometh* and *A Touch of the Poet* did not have New York productions until after World War II ended. The Theatre Guild received both plays from O'Neill in 1944, but production problems ensued and the plays were not suitable for wartime. That year Eugene and Carlotta sold their home in California, finding it too isolated, and went to live in hotels in San Francisco and New York. O'Neill was taking many medications, especially to try and control his tremors and nervous condition, and Carlotta had severe kidney disease.

The Iceman Cometh was first produced on Broadway in 1946, split into two-hour segments with a dinner break. This production was the first new O'Neill play on Broadway in twelve years. Critical reception was widely varied, although many like George Freedley at the *New York Morning Telegraph* said: "*The Iceman Cometh* is first rate O'Neill—Need I say more?"[28] However, spending a whole day at an O'Neill tragedy seemed more than post-war audiences were willing to do, and the show closed after 136 performances. The true possibilities of this play shone forth in 1956, when director Jose Quintero staged it "in-the-round" at an Off-Broadway theatre called Circle in the Square. A landmark performance by Jason Robards Jr. as Hickey, with an outstanding cast, including future star Peter Falk playing the tough bartender Rocky, drew in the crowds. The revival played for 565 performances. Unfortunately O'Neill died before he could see Quintero's work. However, it so pleased Carlotta O'Neill that a year later she chose Quintero to stage her late husband's final masterpiece, *Long Day's Journey Into Night*.

A *Touch of the Poet* did not debut on Broadway until 1958. The splendid cast included British actor Eric Portman and American stage stars Kim Stanley and Helen Hayes as the Melody family. Critics and audiences accepted it favorably, for a solid run of 284 performances.

"May You Rest Forever in Forgiveness and Peace": O'Neill Banishes His Ghosts *Long Day's Journey Into Night* and *A Moon for the Misbegotten*

"My creative energy just balked . . . [it said] 'all is vanity including your plays, past and present, and I am fed up with you and your woes, so good bye and kindly scatter my ashes down the nearest drain.' Then it died."

—Eugene O'Neill to Elizabeth S. Sargeant[1]

The Japanese military bombed Pearl Harbor in 1941, drawing the United States fully into World War II. O'Neill had been laboring over a draft of *A Moon for the Misbegotten*, but soon became obsessed with the death tolls of the war. His passion for writing this play, which would bring his brother Jamie back to life, seemed to fade. In 1940 he had produced a script for *Long Day's Journey Into Night*, the saga of truth-telling spent with his family in Monte Cristo Cottage. Although exhausted from this literary effort, he finally returned to the story of Jamie (called Jim Tyrone) and his relationship with the fictional Hogans.

O'Neill's children caused him grief during this period as well. His daughter, Oona, after attending prep school in New York and joining the débutante set, took off for Los Angeles in 1942 to try acting. Carlotta kept contact at a minimum with Oona, who did indeed try the social and movie scene in Hollywood—and at age eighteen, fell in love with worldwide celebrity actor Charlie Chaplin. Although when he was young, Eugene had pulled plenty of stunts, he never forgave Oona or Chaplin, who was fifty-four at the time, for eloping in 1943.

O'Neill's son Shane had also been a school dropout, and like his father and uncle, became addicted to alcohol. He also tried the dangerous route of drugs. Shane did sign on with the Merchant Marine and fought in 1942. Carlotta was filtering the family mail, so Eugene found out little about him. In 1944, Shane married and produced Eugene O'Neill III, who tragically died of sudden infant death syndrome. Shane did survive a terrible heroin habit, and raised four children, but succumbed to depression and killed himself in 1977.

Eugene Jr. suffered from alcoholism, but managed to hold onto teaching jobs. He and Carlotta shared a mutual hatred for one another, and O'Neill gave in to Carlotta's view of his children. Finally Eugene Jr. ended his life in 1950 by slashing his wrists. Combining the emotional effects of Oona's marriage, Shane's drug habits, and Eugene Jr.'s decline and suicide, O'Neill turned totally to Carlotta for any emotional sustenance. As he wrote and rewrote *Moon* and *Long Day's Journey*, one can only speculate how his unhappy relationships with his children affected his rendering of the Tyrone family in these plays.

Looking back at the twelve themes addressed in O'Neill's first big Broadway hit, *Beyond the Horizon*, in 1920, it is enlightening to see how many he was still exploring in his last great work of the 1940s. Tragedy as part of the ordinary family, self-obsessed protagonists, duty to one's family vs. desire for life abroad, death of marital love, sibling rivalry vs. affection, sons confronting their father, inherited weakness and illness, the place of the poet in society—all are in some way revisited in *Long Day's Journey Into Night*. After thirty years as a dedicated playwright, O'Neill was still trying to solve the great tragic mysteries of life.

A Moon for the Misbegotten received a Theater Guild production in 1947, which sent the show for tryouts in Columbus, Ohio; Pittsburgh, Pennsylvania; Cleveland, Ohio; Detroit, Michigan; and St. Louis, Missouri. The script offended Midwestern audiences and police censors to the point that it was closed in both Detroit and St. Louis. O'Neill published *Moon* as a book in 1952, stating, "I cannot presently give it the attention required for appropriate presentation."[1] The play was never produced again before he died in 1953. O'Neill refused to have *Long Day's Journey Into Night* produced until after his death, feeling it would be too painful to watch his family reconstructed.

Writing these two family-based plays took a great emotional and physical toll on the author. Carlotta O'Neill recorded that her husband often wrote seven to eight hours a day, a grueling schedule for a man with serious debilitating ailments. He still did all his writing while grasping a pen or pencil. After writing, he came out of his study "sometimes weeping. His eyes would be all red and he looked ten years older than when he went in in the morning."[3]

Long Day's Journey Into Night Recreates the Almost-Real O'Neills

As he wrote *Long Day's Journey*, O'Neill described his vision of it in a letter to his close friend George Jean Nathan:

The story of one day, 8 a.m. to midnight,—in the life of a family of four . . . back in 1912 . . . a day in which things occur which evoke the whole past of the family and reveal every aspect of its interrelationships. A deeply tragic play, but without any violent dramatic action. At the final curtain, there they still are, trapped within each other by the past, each guilty and at the same time innocent, scorning, loving, pitying each other, understanding, and yet not understanding at all, forgiving but still doomed never to be able to forget.[4]

Specifically, O'Neill looks at certain themes and symbols in this play. His family was both a supportive and destructive element to him. He needed them, but certainly as a younger man found he could not live with them. Several addictions are explored. James is addicted to accumulating wealth, as he is the sole support of the family and was faced with the Poor House as a boy; Mary through no fault of her own becomes addicted to morphine; Jamie has spent his life addicted to alcohol, perhaps a result of depression and emotional dysfunction stemming from a deep need for his mother; Edmund, who displays a growing drinking problem, is addicted to life as the dependent "baby" of the family.

Time, both a theme and a symbol for the journey of life, is divided into morning, lunchtime, dinnertime, and the dark of midnight. Each quadrant in time shows a progression into the deepening emotional issues the family must face. The title probably refers to the progress of all our long days into that "night"—death itself. The weather underlines these quadrants, as the sun of morning and the heat of noon dissolve into the depressing afternoon fog and the fearful chill of night. There is no turning back real time; yet a trip back through emotional time can be achieved by chemical abuse and personal revelations.

Fog, another often used symbol in O'Neill's plays, here signifies the increasing isolation of the Tyrones both from the community, the world, and from each other.

Problems with maturity and adult responsibility weave through the play, affecting not only the two Tyrone sons but their mother and even their father. Each character is stalled at a certain stage of their development. In real life, the O'Neills did move forward with their addiction issues and their careers. Yet in terms of emotional maturity, all struggled throughout their lives. Faith versus the loss of God is a theme that O'Neill had not addressed so openly in years. Each of the four Tyrones began as faithful Catholics; now the disappearance of God and the Church from their lives has left them struggling to understand their place in the universe.

Setting the play in his family's Monte Cristo Cottage on Pequot Avenue, during the New London summer of 1912, O'Neill gives this work immediate authenticity. On the surface, it seems to be about the Tyrone family spending an uneventful day together. Even if we did not know that the Tyrones (James, Mary, Jamie, and Edmund) represent O'Neill's own family, we would soon guess from the detailed documentary nature of the stage family's activities and revelations. O'Neill made it clear in the dedication of *Long Day's Journey* to his wife Carlotta on their twelfth wedding anniversary, July 22, 1941: "I give you the original script of this play of old sorrow, written in tears and blood. . . . I mean it as a tribute to your love and tenderness which gave me the faith in love that enabled me to face my dead at last and write this play—write it with deep pity and understanding and forgiveness for all the four haunted Tyrones."[5]

Writing a four-family-member work without a primary protagonist or point of view, and being equally, brutally honest

Members of the original *Long Day's Journey Into Night* production visit Monte Cristo Cottage, in New London, Connecticut (l. to r.: Fredrich March (James Tyrone); unidentified production member; Katherine Ross (Cathleen); Jason Robards Jr. (Jamie Tyrone); Florence Eldridge (Mary Tyrone); Bradford Dillman (Edmund); Jose Quintero (director); kneeling: Theodore Mann (producer).

about all four, was a huge challenge for O'Neill. Although Edmund is the young Eugene, the author does not spare the rendering of his faults in the group portrait. All must finally be forgiven their trespasses.

James Tyrone is described physically and professionally in such a way that he is obviously a recreation of James O'Neill Sr. As James attempts to cope with serious problems with his wife and his two sons, his strength starts to crumble. A powerful man who made his way in America after childhood poverty in Ireland, James at age sixty-five is still performing as an actor to support his dependent family. He is proud of his Irish and his Roman Catholic heritage and his success in his self-taught profession.

Mary Tyrone, James's wife, is graceful and pretty at age fifty-four with thick white hair and beautiful brown eyes. As the play progresses, the damage done to Mary by twenty years of injecting morphine, the loss of her father and an infant son, and now terror over losing Edmund, grows evident. She regresses from the present, through a recounting of problems in her marriage, to Edmund's difficult birth and her introduction to morphine; she relives her baby's tragic death, all the way back to her courtship by James, and her girlhood convent days when her father pampered her. Her final monologue leaves her poised in memory as a senior at the convent: "Then in the spring something happened to me. Yes I remember. I fell in love with James Tyrone and was so happy for a time."[6]

point of view

The perspective from which the author tells the story. For example, a story might be told from the point of view of the main character or an unseen narrator.

Jamie Tyrone, at age thirty-three, is the most difficult character to understand. Described as good looking, with romantic Irish charm, Jamie is also an unemployed, desperately depressed alcoholic. His abilities are often lauded, from his brilliance as a student to his prowess as an actor. Yet Jamie is still dependent on handouts from his father, living for the next drink and trip to the brothels of Broadway. His ability to recount stories, recite poetry, and his genuine concern for his mother and brother make Jamie almost appealing, until one realizes the tragic, destructive life he leads.

Edmund Tyrone, although twenty-three years old, seems like a lost teenager. A failure at college, he is now a stringer at the town newspaper. He survived a few sea voyages and writes poems, but has no real career. Jamie sneers at him: "You're only an overgrown kid. Mama's baby and Papa's pet!"[7] Edmund is now at a crossroads in his life. He learns he has "consumption," a form of tuberculosis that killed Mary's father and was often fatal in 1912 (actually the year that Eugene O'Neill came down with the disease). Edmund's doctor states he has a chance for a cure if he spends at least six months at a sanitarium, for which James must pay. With this frightening prospect bowing him down, Edmund must cope with Jamie's sorry assessment of their mother's returning to drugs: "The cures are no . . . good except for while," Jamie tells him. "The truth is there is no cure and we've been saps to hope. They never come back!"[8] If this is true, then Edmund must wonder if going to the tuberculosis sanitarium is hopeless as well.

In O'Neill's "real life," Mary (Ella O'Neill) conquered her morphine addiction before her husband James died of colon cancer. Eugene (Edmund) did spend six months in a treatment facility for tuberculosis and survived the disease. Knowing these facts makes studying this "long day" in the lives of the four Tyrones more intriguing. We realize that O'Neill was not just writing a memoir. He was exploring themes that went beyond his family events into his philosophy of life.

Another friend of Eugene's in his youth was Catholic social activist Dorothy Day. Evenings they spent together talking in Greenwich Village led Day to believe that "Gene's relations with his God was a warfare in itself. He fought with God to the end of his days."[9] The author's spiritual despair is recorded in *Long Day's Journey*, Act II. Although James admits that he is "a bad Catholic in the observance," he declares he prays daily. Edmund asks, "Did you pray for Mama?" James replies, "I did. I prayed these many years for her." Edmund states, "Then Nietzsche must be right. 'God is dead: of His pity for man hath God died.'"[10]

Some critics state that O'Neill uses the Roman Catholic sacrament of confession (or penance) throughout the play as each character accuses others, but confesses their own faults and transgressions. Laurin Porter notes that the Tyrones' confessions "hold out hope that the cycle of recrimination can be broken. . . . Confessing one's sins to a representative of God who is authorized to wipe the slate clean and reestablish harmony with the cosmos is a ritual that recapitulates Christ's mediation between God and man."[11] However, most of the confessions are made to Edmund. While they help him better understand the rationale behind his family's treatment of each other, Edmund is no priest. Of all of them, he is the least in tune with God. Porter says: "As the curtain rings down, the Tyrones remain locked in time; nothing has changed."[12]

Long Day's Journey opened in Stockholm in February 1956 to overall approval. Carlotta O'Neill contracted Jose Quintero from the Circle in the Square (who had done *The Iceman Cometh*) to stage the play on November 7, 1956, on

Broadway. Cast members Frederick March, Florence Eldridge, Jason Robards Jr., and Bradford Dillman were experienced, outstanding actors.

Brooks Atkinson of the *New York Times* saw beyond autobiography to the "universal and tragic truths."[13] Although Atkinson could not decide if the play was O'Neill's greatest, he said it ranked with his finest. Henry Hewes of the *Saturday Review* called it "the most universal piece of stage realism ever turned out by an American playwright."[14] However, not every New York critic praised the work. Some critics complained about its repetition and length. O'Neill did indeed use repetition—as he did in other works—to give the feeling that these characters were repeating stories, accusations, and excuses that they had each heard a hundred times in the past. As for length, O'Neill has probably gone down in history as America's most long-winded playwright. Yet in this case, length was almost essential to portray the feeling of endlessness to the family's twenty four-hour ordeal. Walter Kerr of the *Herald-Tribune* summed it up well when he said the play was deliberately and masochistically harrowing. Kerr said seeing the play is "an obligation for anyone who cares about the theatre. It is a stun ning theatrical experience."[15] His estimation has proven to be true, for this work must be considered O'Neill's triumphant, most revived play. The play was awarded the 1956 Pulitzer Prize for drama posthumously, after his death in November 1953. This made O'Neill a four-time winner.

O'Neill's Farewell to Brother Jim:
A Moon for the Misbegotten

The decline of Jamie O'Neill (known as Jim by the rest of the world) haunted Eugene for the rest of his life. One of the excuses that both Jamie and Eugene used for being drunkards was the nightmare of their mother's drug addiction. Ella O'Neill removed that excuse when she successfully kicked the habit in 1914.

Ella's personal recovery did not stop her sons from drinking. Both alcoholics since their teen years, Jamie and Eugene often used alcohol as an aid in communicating with each other. After his parents died, Eugene tried psychoanalysis to help him with depression and addiction. Jamie grew angrier, ever more distant and jealous of his brother, and refused treatment for alcoholism. Their estrangement lasted until Jamie's death in 1923. Eugene continued to drink through 1925, at which point it was affecting his writing and his marriage. In early 1926, a psychiatrist was able to help, allowing Eugene the tools to analyze and monitor himself. Eugene went into recovery and drank only episodically for the rest of his life.

How Eugene O'Neill dealt with decades of unresolved resentment and anger toward his brother, Jamie, is impossible to say. However, by creating the characters of Jamie Tyrone in *Long Day's Journey* and Jim Tyrone in *A Moon for the Misbegotten*, O'Neill worked through what analysts call a process of separation and mourning. Jim Tyrone of *Moon* becomes for O'Neill a walking ghost.

Josie Hogan at age twenty-eight has been a surrogate mother to her three brothers, for their own mother died at the youngest boy's birth. The opening description of Josie is "oversize" (for a woman of 1928) at five feet eleven inches tall, extremely strong, black-haired, blue-eyed, Irish to the core, "all woman." As she bids farewell to her youngest brother Mike, she knows her life running the hardscrabble farm without help will be a tough one. Mike advises her to shape up and get away from their scheming, lazy father: "You ought to marry and have a home of your own away from this shanty and stop your shameless ways.[16] Josie desires Jim Tyrone, but says: "A big ugly hulk like me . . . if he ever was tempted to want me, he'd be ashamed of it."[17]

Phil Hogan, fifty-five, stocky, a coarse, crude but sometimes amusing Irishman, is Josie's father. A sloppy pig farmer, Hogan spent years trying to con the senior Tyrone into lower rent, but knows he must get around Jim Tyrone to hold onto the place. The two of them are "players in an old familiar game where each knows the other's moves."[18] A grafter and drinker, Hogan fears he may be in trouble without his sons for laborers.

Many of O'Neill's characters struggled with alcoholism, as did he and members of his family. O'Neill was known to frequent this New York City bar, the Golden Swan Cafe.

Jim Tyrone is described just before his first entrance by Josie "like a dead man walking slow behind his own coffin. Faith, he must have a hangover."[19] In his early forties, good looking but dissipated from drink, Jim has "the ghost of a former youthful, irresponsible Irish charm."[20] By the end of the long first act, we see that Jim and Josie are genuinely fond of each other—as much as Jim can care for any woman. Severe guilt eats at him. The Broadway dandy and the farmer's daughter will love—but lose.

A Moon for the Misbegotten becomes a play of misconceptions, misdirection, and missed opportunities. Josie is trying to hold onto what she has and move ahead into a future that hopefully includes Jim. Jim is stuck heading back through the past—the past tragedy of his behavior at his mother's death, and the meaning of his place as an Irish American. Although Jim is the Yankee son of an Irishman who made money, he does not side with the oil-rich neighbor Stedman Harder but hangs back with the low-class Irish Hogans. He has promised never to sell Harder the farm.

The major conflict of the plot is between Josie and Jim. Fearing Jim has lied about selling the farm, Josie turns against him. But when he finally shows up for their "date" after having gotten drunk at the Inn, Jim says he left because "I was going batty alone there. The old heebie-jeebies. So I came to you.—I've really begun to love you a lot, Josie."[21] When Josie embraces Jim, O'Neill states: "She stares down at his face with a passionate, possessive tenderness."[22]

What are Jim's heebie-jeebies? Does Jim need Josie as a lover or a mother? And what is generating his guilt—lust, lies, or a past misdeed? Jim insists: "You can take the truth, Josie— from me. Because you and I belong to the same club. We can kid the world but we can't fool ourselves."[23] Self-honesty will become their path.

Jim's final series of speeches constitutes a dizzying portrayal of a man so torn inside that he flashes from present to past, from lusty seducer to lover to son, from drunk to truth-teller and back, trying to outrun his pain. When Josie offers herself and tells him, "I'll have had tonight and your love to remember for the rest of my days," Jim becomes the Broadway prostitute monger and snaps: "Come on, Baby Doll! Let's hit the hay."[24] Again, Jim pleads "the old heebie jeebies," now causing him to see "a blonde pig" in Josie's place. Leading into the confession of what he did to his mother, and perhaps his younger brother, Jim says, "Believe me, Kid, when I poison them they stay poisoned."[25]

The dead man inside Jim results from failing to honor his vow to his dying mother to stay sober. "She saw I was drunk," he tells Josie. "Then she closed her eyes so she couldn't see, and was glad to die."[26] His train trip across the country with his mother's corpse in the baggage car and a prostitute and a bottle in his compartment put Jim in such a state of guilt that he is now on the road to self-destruction.

The moon goes down, dawn breaks, and during Act IV O'Neill must explore what paths Jim Tyrone, Josie, and Phil Hogan will travel after this experience. Jim kisses Josie, telling her he will never forget the love she gave him that night: "I'll always love you, Josie. Goodbye—and God bless you!"[27] As Jim leaves, Josie weeps for him and the relationship she cannot give her. Her curtain line tells us: "May you have your wish and die in your sleep soon, Jim, darling. May you rest forever in forgiveness and peace."[28]

Scholar Travis Bogard wrote that this curtain line is the benediction O'Neill wanted to give to his three deceased family members: "These were the last words O'Neill was to write for the stage and they express what came in the end to be the consummation of his tragedy."[29] In reality, Jamie O'Neill never had the simple love of a Josie Hogan to send him on to the next life. In the eternity of literature, his brother Eugene gave him this blessing and laid him to rest. Bogard recalled O'Neill's dedication to *Long Day's Journey* when he said, "Bringing peace to Jamie meant by extension bringing peace to all the four haunted Tyrones."[30]

A Moon for the Misbegotten did not gain instant acceptance in New York during its 1957 run. Critics claimed it was over-written, tedious, and uneven. Brooks Atkinson at the *New York Times* said it lacked "O'Neill's elemental power."[31] Others saw its haunting emotional undercurrents, and Walter Kerr called the last act "a superb dance of death." The play did become a highly regarded piece after its 1973 revival. Critic Elyse Sommer said of this production: "(Coleen) Dewhurst and (Jason) Robards rescued O'Neill's failed play from neglect by digging beneath the facades these desperate people presented to the world."[32]

Summing up this study of O'Neill's major dramas, we can see that he faced the nobility of life's struggle and the darkness of death in each one. Characters seen and unseen either take their own lives, or the lives of others, the death total surpassing sixteen victims. O'Neill's personal experience with suicide (attempted or successful) in his extended family and close friends included his grandfather, his mother, his two male friends, his son—and himself. It is easy to see the experiences O'Neill brought to his work in becoming America's foremost author of tragic drama.

"THE FATHER OF US ALL": O'NEILL LIVES INTO THE 21ST CENTURY

"I would just say that I find a lot more to agree with in O'Neill's vision than to disagree . . . it's pretty hard not to look outside yourself and feel bleak. I'm not as dark as O'Neill, thank God. But I have my dark moments."

—Actor Brian Dennehy on his decades of work in seven O'Neill revivals[1]

Films Keep O'Neill's Work Accessible

Apparently Eugene O'Neill never involved himself in the screenplays of his works. After MGM made *Strange Interlude* into a film in 1932, O'Neill stated: "Outside of money . . . nothing they do or don't do seems of the slightest importance to my work as a playwright."[2] Fortunately for his legion of fans throughout the world, O'Neill and his wives enjoyed the money enough to turn over many of O'Neill's best plays to filmmakers. Film critic Leonard Maltin serves as the record keeper as we note five films of O'Neill's work.

1. *Anna Christie* was made into a silent film starring Blanche Sweet in 1923. It was then chosen to be the first talking film for Greta Garbo in 1930. Garbo filmed two versions: the

Clark Gable and Norma Shearer starred in the 1932 film version of *Strange Interlude*. The movie was shortened from the play's original running time of more than four hours.

English one featuring herself as Anna, Clarence Brown as Chris, and Charles Bickford as Burke the sailor; she starred in it again in a German version, which Maltin says "is treated in a much more frank and adult way than the Hollywood film."[3]

2. *Strange Interlude* opened on Broadway on January 30, 1928, and ran for nearly two years, making it a bona fide hit. The film did not come out until 1932, with a marvelous cast starring Norma Shearer as Nina, featuring Clark Gable, Robert Young, and Ralph Morgan. Maltin called it engrossing, although the marathon of inner thoughts seemed talky.

3. *The Emperor Jones* became one of the most unusual versions of O'Neill on film. First presented in 1920, the play depended on staging effects to create the emotional regression and fears that Brutus Jones endures. Script adaptor DuBose Heyward expanded the story in 1933 to include much imagined prehistory in Jones's life, which highlighted the musical ability of its new star, Paul Robeson. Jones's character goes from a humble southern church-going lad to wild, crap-shooting man about Manhattan to murderer of a man who threatened his woman to a chain gang escapee, singing all the way. Once he lands on the Caribbean island (where the play began), Robeson brings out Jones's ruthlessness and bleeds the natives. Although the style and dialect appears today to be condescending to blacks, Robeson makes his character believable, insufferably proud, and truly tragic.

4. *Mourning Becomes Electra* was released in 1947 and directed by Dudley Nichols. This lengthy four-hour play was cut to run 159 minutes in England and only 105 minutes in America. The stars who portrayed the Mannons and their lovers were Rosalind Russell, Katina Paxinou, Michael Redgrave, Raymond Massey, and Kirk Douglas. Russell and Redgrave received Academy Award nominations.

5. *Long Day's Journey Into Night* was filmed to run almost three hours, a faithful version of the stage play. Actors Katharine Hepburn, Ralph Richardson, Jason Robards, and Dean Stockwell were critically acclaimed in this 1962 film. Other versions were made for television.

Successors Credit O'Neill's Influence

In the 1940s when Eugene O'Neill was writing his last great works, two younger men had studied his achievements. Thomas "Tennessee" Williams (1911–1983) and Arthur Miller (1915–2005) were breaking into Broadway theatre with dramas that were influenced by many of O'Neill's major themes and concerns.

Tennessee Williams

When Tennessee Williams did his last year in the University of Iowa Theatre Department, he wrote his senior term paper on the O'Neill plays that he could find in print. Professor Philip Kolin recalled how Williams admired O'Neill.[4] Williams's breakthrough drama *The Glass Menagerie* arrived on Broadway in 1945, meaning Williams could have seen *The Iceman Cometh* which had a Broadway run in 1946. When his drama *A Streetcar Named Desire* won the Pulitzer in 1948, O'Neill's sea plays were revived at New York City Center. During *Anna Christie's* revival in January 1952, William's *The Rose Tattoo* was the Tony Award winner. And when *Desire Under the Elms* had its revival in late 1952, Williams's *Summer and Smoke* ran at the same time. It is likely Williams attended all the O'Neill dramas.

Williams became interested in the modern female psyche, as well as interior monologues, symbolism, regression from present time into past experiences, the poet/hero against the corporate world, and most importantly, the need for illusion and dreams to handle the hardship of life. All these elements were apparent in O'Neill's dramas, as well as their common sources of August Strindberg and Henrik Ibsen. Williams transferred them into his creation of the Wingfield family in *The Glass Menagerie*. When Williams wrote about another family, that of Blanche and Stella DuBois and Stella's husband, Stanley, in *A Streetcar Named Desire*, he used many elements in common with *The Iceman Cometh*. Blanche must survive through self-delusion and alcohol, when she portrays herself

Tennessee Williams admired O'Neill's work and included similar elements in many of his own plays.

as a pure, aristocratic Southern belle—but finds she can't keep up this false image on the inside. Like the men in *Iceman*, she subsists on pipe dreams, until her brother-in-law Stanley finds out the truth. The systematic stripping of illusions is done brutally in both plays, until both Blanche and Hickey appear to have lost their lifelines to the real world.

Williams continued to express his respect for O'Neill's work. In a 1956 interview, he stated, "O'Neill gave birth to the American theatre and died for it."[5] He told Dotson Rader in 1981, "I liked O'Neill's writing . . . he had a great sense of drama, yes. But most of all it was his spirit, his passion that moved me." [6] He was so moved that he painted one of his few portraits, entitled "Homage to Eugene O'Neill," which hangs in Columbia University's Rare Book and Manuscript Library.

Arthur Miller

Miller was interested in O'Neill's style, but not so much in his characters or content, until he realized that like himself, deep down O'Neill favored socialism. Miller stated he saw the 1946 production of *The Iceman Cometh* as he was writing his own drama *All My Sons.* The wide array of characters taking their refuge in Harry Hope's Saloon represented every social issue in American society. Somehow O'Neill wove their fates together, in a way that Miller tried to emulate. Hickey, the traveling salesman with questionable honesty and morals, was in some ways reflected in Willie, the hero of Miller's next play, *Death of a Salesman*, which opened in 1949.

O'Neill's obsession with father-son relationships was picked up by Miller in both *All My Sons* and *Salesman.* Miller also made use of O'Neill's stage devices, such as hearing and speaking to people from the past who only exist for the protagonist and the audience. Miller set his play *The Crucible*

Arthur Miller was another great playwright who was influenced not only by O'Neill's technique but also his worldviews.

(1952), a study of the individual against authority, in early New England. This use of past settings worked well for O'Neill in many of his plays. Miller made his own successful attempt to transfer Greek tragedy to the American stage in *A View from the Bridge* (1955). *Desire Under the Elms* and *Mourning Becomes Electra* can be seen as predecessors to this dark urban tragedy of a Sicilian laborer named Eddie, who develops an illicit, maddening passion for his young niece. Betraying both his wife and his obligation to protect his Sicilian family, Eddie even gives up his niece's boyfriend to keep her for himself.

New O'Neill Fans Attend Revivals

Many of O'Neill's dramas have attracted new enthusiasts to attend stage revivals, mostly performed in America and Great Britain.

The Sea Plays—O'Neill's short plays titled *Bound East for Cardiff, In the Zone,* and *The Long Voyage Home*—go back to the beginning of his career in 1914–1918. Their vitality remained as the men sailed the ship of life in London's Old Vic Tunnels in 2012. This odd performance space, discovered by Kevin Spacey under Waterloo Station, seemed perfect for a group of men, often lost in the fog, struggling to make it home. Critic Dominic Cavendish wrote, "these formative years leave their mark on O'Neill's major plays."[7]

The 1974 production of *A Moon for the Misbegotten,* which many critics say could not be beat, starred Jason Robards, Colleen Dewhurst, and Ed Flanders, and it is available on video. Broadway saw a fresh revival of the play on April 10, 2007, that transferred from London's Old Vic Theatre Company. Artistic Director Kevin Spacey played Jim, with England's Eve Best and Colm Meaney playing Josie and Phil.

A marquee announces the 2007 Broadway production of *A Moon for the Misbegotten* starring Kevin Spacey and Eve Best.

The Hairy Ape was revived by the Irish Repertory Theatre and played New York in October 2006. It was again revived at London's Old Vic in 2015. Termed an anti-capitalist drama, critic Susannah Clapp was excited to see the production "storming into the theatre, with a blazing performance from Bertie Carvel, and an unforgettable frieze of images."[8] She does criticize the audibility, yet says there was never any doubt about what is being felt.

Ah, Wilderness! is often revived in regional and community theatres. A recent production in the fall of 2015 lit up the San Francisco scene, staged by the American Conservatory Theatre.

Mourning Becomes Electra is surely one of the most challenging of O'Neill's tragedies to restage. Critic Matt Wolf for *Variety* reviewed the London 2003–2004 production, saying it "maintains its sobriety through to its terrifying final image" and meets O'Neill "fully attuned to the majesty of what just may be the most merciless of all his works."[9] Stars Helen Mirren as Christine and Eve Best as Lavinia received raves.

repertory theatre

A regional theatre that is nonprofit, produces limited runs of plays, and is devoted more to quality artistic work than commercial success.

Two recent revivals of *Long Day's Journey Into Night* received critical acclaim. Critic Charles Isherwood reviewed the Broadway revival of 2003, and called it a "brooding masterpiece about the pain of forgiving and the impossibility of forgetting."[10] He praised Vanessa Redgrave's playing of Mary Tyrone as "the primary revelation of the evening and the season . . . This is truly a woman in the grip of addiction." Redgrave is brilliantly balanced by Brian Dennehy's acting as James Tyrone, "distinguished by its intelligent understatement."

The second revival of *Long Day's Journey* in London in 2012 found unusual casting in Laurie Metcalf and David Suchet. Both performers, known for their work on television, received outstanding critical reviews, moving perfectly into the skins of James and Mary Tyrone. Michael Billington, critic for *The Guardian*, praises Suchet's multifaceted playing of James, especially noting his "forlorn passion for his wife, when he tells her 'it is you who are leaving us,' his voice fills with a sorrowful resignation that stops the heart."[11]

Major Interpreters Return to O'Neill

Several actors have had their greatest successes in portraying the leads in O'Neill revivals. The late Jason Robards, Brian Dennehy, and Gabriel Byrne have done multiple revivals of major leads. Dennehy, also known for his work in film, has scored Broadway raves for his 1990 production of *The Iceman Cometh*, playing Hickey, followed by his 1996 rendering of Con Melody in *A Touch of the Poet*. He returned to Broadway in 2003 to win the Tony Award for his portrayal of James Tyrone in *Long Day's Journey Into Night*. Dennehy played the starring role in *Hughie* in 2004 and 2010. When the Goodman (Chicago's premier regional theatre) celebrated O'Neill with "A Global Exploration: Eugene O'Neill in the 21st Century," Dennehy headlined the festival in a revival of *Desire Under the Elms*, which transferred to Broadway. The Goodman's production of *The Iceman Cometh*, first run in 2012, then transferred to New York in 2015, featured Dennehy as Larry Slade the anarchist.

When interviewed in 2015 by Alexis Soloski, Dennehy talked about his thirty-year passion for O'Neill. In the early 1970s, he acted in O'Neill's sea plays: "His wonderful dialogue, his wonderful characters are there. It was like being infected with some longterm virus. As an Irish American, it's pretty hard to resist O'Neill."[12] Dennehy recalled talking to author Arthur Miller about O'Neill, who said he was "the deep diver. He was the guy who went down. He wanted to find out what the soul was all about . . . he went to places that no other writer has ever gone to. He was a philosopher of the soul."

Gabriel Byrne, a well-known Irish film and TV star, seems to save his best stage performances for O'Neill plays. Byrne starred in the 2000 revival of *A Moon for the Misbegotten* on Broadway, and received the Tony nomination. In 2005–06 he gave a memorable performance as Con Melody in *A Touch of the Poet*. At this printing, Byrne is scheduled to open as James Tyrone with Jessica Lange in *Long Day's Journey Into Night* in the spring of 2016.

Forest Whitaker will make his Broadway debut of O'Neill's one-act *Hughie* at the same time. *Hughie*, an hour-long, two-character play, was written in the spring of 1941, after O'Neill completed *Long Day's Journey Into Night*. It is thought to be his final complete work, and was produced through the 1960s and has often been revived.

Fifty Years of Training the Playwrights, Critics, Artists and Performers of Tomorrow

In the summer of 1966, a California college student arrived at the fledgling Eugene O'Neill Theater Center in Waterford, Connecticut. Intern Michael Douglas recalled: "I was responsible for lawn mowing and facilities maintenance. In between carving out a new amphitheatre next to an old barn, I began working with incredible playwrights, directors, and actors . . . with work so inspiring that I spent the next two summers there too."[13] Looking back, Michael Douglas states, "I would not be who or where I am today without the O'Neill."

Hundreds of plays and musicals have been launched here at the Eugene O'Neill Theater Center in Waterford, Connecticut.

He also recalled meeting a short, snappy teen from New York named Danny DeVito, and while learning to become actors, the boys got into a fair amount of mischief.

Another major player in the American theatre made her way through Yale School of Drama, and by 1975 was also interning at the O'Neill Theater Center. Meryl Streep's memories are of "the actors, directors, dramaturgs, and administrators, dreamers all."[14] She fondly recalled working with her fellow players Christopher Lloyd, Jill Eikenberry, and actor-director Joe Grifisi, who have enjoyed great careers. "We were all engaged in full-hearted passion . . . in the service of finding that wiggly elusive creature, a new play."[15] Streep learned to go with her first instincts, due to their time constraints: "That's what actors at the O'Neill did, with full-blown commitment. It's a good lesson. One I've carried with me my whole life."[16]

The Eugene O'Neill Theater Center is a non-profit institution that helps developing theatre students, professional playwrights, composers, puppeteers, and critics learn their art and craft. This institution works for the future of the American theatre, just as Eugene O'Neill would have wished. It was founded by George C. White, a native of Waterford and an alumni of the Yale University School of Drama. White had an inspiration: why not make a waterside property owned by the community into a summer theatre institute for Yale? When Yale reneged but the Town of Waterford voted yes, White forged ahead. He received permission from a delighted Carlotta Monterey O'Neill to name the center after Eugene O'Neill: "Could he know this," she wrote, "he would be more than pleased. . . May you have even greater success than you expect."[17]

The programs of the O'Neill Theater Center are as follows: the National Playwrights Conference offers authors a month to develop their new work through staged script-in-hand readings; the Music Theater Conference brings in composing and writing teams to develop new musicals with professional singer/actors and musical directors; the Puppetry Conference explores new frontiers with puppet artists, playwrights, and directors; the National Critics Institute provides one week for professional theatre critics to share information, critical feedback, and the actual backstage experience of producing a show; and the National Theater Institute is an accredited college training program for students in acting, directing, and designing. College students apply for the six-week summer "Theatermakers" as well as full-semester programs each summer and fall. All program entrants are selected by a competitive application process.

The National Music Theatre Conference kept O'Neill's work directly alive by workshopping an opera version of *Desire Under the Elms* in 1979. It received a world premiere by the New York Opera Repertory Theatre at City Center in 1989.[18]

The Monte Cristo Cottage at 325 Pequot Avenue in New London is also managed by the Center. It is open to the public as a house museum. O'Neill family portraits and photos of New London taken during O'Neill's youth are displayed.[19] It is also used for a very special purpose: to infuse students with the true pioneering soul of Eugene O'Neill. Each class of NTI students sits in the cottage front parlor and reads aloud the entire script of *Long Day's Journey Into Night*. This front parlor was used not only as the set for this play, but also for *Ah, Wilderness!*.

Director Robert Falls was preparing a production of *Long Day's Journey Into Night* for a Broadway production in the spring of 2003. Although he had visited the Monte Cristo Cottage before, he wanted his cast members to experience its ambience. So he brought Brian Dennehy, Vanessa Redgrave, Philip Seymour Hoffman, and Robert Sean Leonard to the house. "They opened the house to us," he recalled. "We read the play until about one in the morning."[20] Vanessa Redgrave explored the space, climbed the stairway, the other actors following her. The cast realized that the house is truly a claustrophobic space and the floors did creak. "You really do get kind of connected with the ghosts that were in that house," said Falls.[21]

The Board of the Eugene O'Neill Theater Center decided in 2000 to present a "Monte Cristo Award" to an individual whose career in the American theatre personified O'Neill's pioneering spirit. The first award went to actor Jason Robards, who had performed great revivals on stage, TV, and film of O'Neill plays since the 1950s. Other recipients include (in alphabetical order) Edward Albee, Zoe Caldwell, Brian Dennehy, Michael Douglas, Arthur and Barbara Gelb, James Earl Jones, Karl Malden, Christopher Plummer, Harold Prince, Neil Simon, Kevin Spacey, Meryl Streep, Wendy Wasserstein, and August Wilson. The most recent recipient is Nathan Lane.

The Tony Award for Best Regional Theatre was given to the O'Neill Theatre Center in 2010. As Carlotta Monterey O'Neill said in the beginning, Eugene would be more than pleased.

O'Neill: The Playwright Gets the Last Word

Eugene O'Neill once said, "The theatre should reveal to us who we are."[22] It should give us "a better understanding of ourselves and a better understanding of one another." He summed up his view of life in 1923 by saying, "I see life as a gorgeously-ironical, beautifully-indifferent, splendidly-suffering bit of chaos the tragedy of which gives Man a tremendous significance. . . . I'm no pessimist. On the contrary, I'm tickled to death with life! I wouldn't 'go out' and miss the rest of the play for anything!"[23]

CHRONOLOGY

1877— James O'Neill Sr. marries Mary Ellen (Ella) Quinlan.

1878— James O'Neill Jr. is born; he is called Jamie.

1883— Edmund O'Neill is born.

1885— Edmund dies of measles.

1888— Eugene O'Neill is born on October 16 in New York City.

1895— Attends the Academy of Mount St. Vincent, a boarding school in Riverdale, New York.

1900— Attends Betts Academy in Stamford, Connecticut.

1906— Enters Princeton University but fails out in 1907.

1909— Marries Kathleen Jenkins.

1910— Eugene G. O'Neill Jr. is born. Eugene O'Neill becomes a sailor.

1911 O'Neill returns to New York; he is an alcoholic and attempts suicide.

1912— Lives at the family summer home in New London, Connecticut, and works on the local newspaper; divorces Kathleen Jenkins.

1913— Develops tuberculosis and is treated in Wallingford, Connecticut; starts writing plays.

1914— Attends playwriting class at Harvard; publishes his first one-acts.

1916— Moves to Provincetown, Massachusetts, where his short plays are produced.

1917— Has more plays produced in Provincetown and Greenwich Village; falls in love with writer Agnes Boulton.

1918— Marries Agnes; three more of his short plays are produced.

1919— O'Neill and Agnes's son Shane O'Neill is born; one of Eugene's plays is produced.

1920– Full-length modern tragedy, *Beyond the Horizon*, is produced and wins the Pulitzer Prize for drama; James O'Neill Sr. dies of cancer; *The Emperor Jones* is produced.

1921– *Anna Christie* is produced and wins the Pulitzer Prize for drama; two of his short plays are produced.

1922– Ella O'Neill dies of a stroke; *The Hairy Ape* and another short play by O'Neill are produced; Jamie O'Neill suffers from acute alcoholism.

1923– Jamie O'Neill, estranged from his family, dies.

1924– *All God's Chillun Got Wings*, *Desire Under the Elms*, and a short play are produced.

1925– Play, *The Fountain*, is produced; daughter Oona is born.

1926– *The Great God Brown* is produced.

1928– *Lazarus Laughed* is produced in Pasadena, California; *Marco Millions* and *Strange Interlude* are produced in New York; *Strange Interlude* wins O'Neill's third Pulitzer Prize for drama; O'Neill separates from Agnes.

1929– *Dynamo* is produced; O'Neill divorces Agnes; marries Carlotta Monterey in Paris.

1930– O'Neill writes and lives in Europe with Carlotta.

1931– *Mourning Becomes Electra* is produced.

1933– *Ah, Wilderness!* is produced.

1934– *Days Without End* is produced.

1936– Awarded the Nobel Prize for Literature.

1937– O'Neill and Carlotta build a home, Tao House, in Danville, California.

1938– O'Neill's health begins to decline.

1939– Writes *The Iceman Cometh*; he also drafts *More Stately Mansions*, a work that he will never revise for stage production.

1940– Writes *Long Day's Journey Into Night*.

1942–1943– Writes *A Moon for the Misbegotten*.

1946– *The Iceman Cometh* is produced.

1947– *A Moon for the Misbegotten* is produced in Columbus, Ohio, but fails.

1950– O'Neill's health worsens; son Eugene O'Neill Jr. commits suicide.

1953– Eugene G. O'Neill dies on November 27 in Boston. The cause, later determined, is pneumonia brought on by weakness due to spinal cerebellar atrophy. He is buried in Forest Hills Cemetery, Boston, Massachusetts.

1955– *The Iceman Cometh* is revived successfully in New York. Its 565 performances are a record for an O'Neill Broadway play.

1956– *Long Day's Journey Into Night* is produced in Stockholm and then in New York; it wins O'Neill's fourth Pulitzer Prize, the Drama Circle Critics Award, and the Tony.

1957– *A Moon for the Misbegotten* premieres on Broadway.

1958– *A Touch of the Poet* is produced in New York. O'Neill's *Hughie*, a short play, is produced in Stockholm; it premiers in New York in 1964. *Desire Under the Elms* finally gets a film version.

1958– O'Neill's *Hughie*, a short play, is produced in Stockholm. It premiers in New York in 1964. *Desire Under the Elms* finally gets a film version.

1959– The Eugene O'Neill Theatre on 49th Street in New York City is opened, honoring O'Neill's name.

1966– The Eugene O'Neill Theater Center opens in Waterford, Connecticut. The non-profit institution will help develop playwrights, theatre students, puppeteers, and drama critics. Tao House, O'Neill's home from 1937–1944 outside Danville, California, opens to the public as part of the Eugene O'Neill

Foundation. It is taken over by the National Park Service and now includes performances and related educational programs.

1968— Agnes Boulton O'Neill dies from severe alcoholism.

1970— Carlotta O'Neill is hospitalized for a nervous breakdown in 1968. She dies in November 1970.

1971— Monte Cristo Cottage, O'Neill's family home in New London, Connecticut, receives National Historic Landmark status.

1972— Curators begin to restore Monte Cristo Cottage, a project of the O'Neill Theater Center.

1977— Son Shane O'Neill commits suicide.

1979— Eugene O'Neill Society formally organizes to promote and maintain worldwide study of O'Neill's works. The Society publishes the *Eugene O'Neill Review* and holds periodic international conferences, the most recent being in New York in 2011.

1982— Monte Cristo Cottage opens to the public as a house museum.

1986— "Eugene O'Neill: A Glory of Ghosts" airs on PBS, directed by Perry Miller Adato.

2000— The Board of the Eugene O'Neill Theater Center presents the Monte Cristo Award to an individual whose career in the theatre personifies O'Neill's pioneering spirit. The first award goes to actor Jason Robards.

2006— *Eugene O'Neill: A Documentary Film*, directed by Ric Burns, is released on PBS's *American Experience* and on DVD.

2010— The Eugene O'Neill Theater Center receives the Tony Award for Best Regional Theater.

CHAPTER NOTES

Chapter 1. Backstage Baby to Broadway Playwright

1. Eugene O'Neill to Mary Ann Clark, August 8, 1923, in Stephen A. Black, *Eugene O'Neill: Beyond Mourning and Tragedy* (New Haven, CT: Yale University Press, 1999), vii.
2. Robert M. Dowling, *Eugene O'Neill: A Life in Four Acts* (New Haven, CT: Yale University Press, 2014), 9.
3. Jackson R. Bryer and Robert M. Dowling, eds., *Eugene O'Neill: The Contemporary Reviews* (New York: Cambridge University Press, 2014), 9.
4. Travis Bogard and Jackson R. Byers, eds., *Selected Letters of Eugene O'Neill* (New Haven, CT: Yale University Press, 1988), 113.
5. Byer and Dowling, 67.
6. Ibid., 84.
7. *Eugene O'Neill: Complete Plays, 1913–1920*, The Library of America (New York: Literary Classics of the United States, 1988), 576.
8. Ibid., 597.
9. Ibid., 577.
10. Ibid., 616.
11. Ibid.5, 592.
12. Croswell Bowen, "The Black Irishman," *PM Magazine*, Nov. 3, 1946, in Mark Estrin, ed., *Conversations with Eugene O'Neill* (Jackson, MS: University Press of Mississippi, 1990), 204.
13. Ibid., 204.
14. *Eugene O'Neill: Complete Plays, 1913–1920*, 616.
15. Ibid., 653.
16. Arthur Gelb and Barbara Gelb, *O'Neill: Life With Monte Cristo* (New York: Applause Books, 2002), 638.

Chapter 2. "I've Knocked About a Bit": O'Neill's Rough Youth Reflected in Early Works

1. Travis Bogard and Jackson R. Bryer, eds., *Selected Letters of Eugene O'Neill* (New Haven, CT: Yale University Press, 1988), 118.

2. Stephen A. Black, *Eugene O'Neill: Beyond Mourning and Tragedy* (New Haven, CT: Yale University Press, 1999), 44.

3. Louis Sheaffer, *O'Neill: Son and Playwright* (New York: Cooper Square Press, 2002), 40.

4. Ibid., 41.

5. Ibid., 59.

6. Arthur Gelb and Barbara Gelb, *O'Neill* (New York: Harper & Row, 1973), 68.

7. Ibid., 81.

8. Sheaffer, 116.

9. Ibid., 120.

10. Bogard and Bryer, 477.

11. Sheaffer, 133.

12. Barrett H. Clark, *Eugene O'Neill: The Man and His Plays* (New York: Dover, 1947), 15.

13. Ibid., 21.

14. Michiko Kakutani, "Hospital Remembers Rebirth of O'Neill," *The New York Times*, November 18, 1982, www.nytimes.com/1982/10/1/theater/hospital-remembers-rebirth-of-o-neill.html.

Chapter 3. From Small Plays a Full-Blown Hit Will Grow

1. George Cram "Jig" Cook, in Robert M. Dowling, *Eugene O'Neill, A Life in Four Acts*, (New Haven, CT: Yale University Press, 2014), 146.

2. Susan Glaspell in *The Provincetown: A Story of the Theatre,* Helen Deutsch and Stella Hanau (New York: Farrar & Rinehart, 1931), 12.

3. Eugene O'Neill, *The Plays of Eugene O'Neill* (New York: Random House, 1964), 1:629.

4. Ibid., 632.

5. Stephen A. Black, *Eugene O'Neill: Beyond Mourning and Tragedy* (New Haven, CT: Yale University Press, 1999), 200.

6. *The Plays of Eugene O'Neill,* 578.

7. Ibid.

8. Ibid., 592.

9. Ibid., 611.

10. Ibid., 615.

11. Arthur Gelb and Barbara Gelb, *O'Neill* (New York: Random House, 1964), 439.

12. Eugene O'Neill, *Nine Plays by Eugene O'Neill* (New York: The Modern Library, 1952), 33.

13. Ibid., 34.

14. Eugene O'Neill to Malcolm Cowley, "O'Neill: Writer of Synthetic Drama, 1926," in Mark W. Estrin, ed., *Conversations with Eugene O'Neill* (Jackson, MS: University Press of Mississippi, 1990), 79.

15. Gelb and Gelb, 447.

16. Glenda Frank, "'The Emperor Jones' by Eugene O'Neill," eOneill.com, 2006, www.eoncill.com/reviews/jones_frank.htm.

17. *The Plays of Eugene O'Neill,* 3:18.

18. Ibid., 28–29.

19. Ibid., 74.

20. "O'Neill's reply to critics," *The New York Times,* December 18, 1921.

21. Ibid.

22. Conversation with Malcolm Mollan, in Estrin, 15.

Chapter 4. Capitalism, Race, and Lust for Land: O'Neill Explores New Themes

1. Robert M. Dowling, *Eugene O'Neill: A Life in Four Acts* (New Haven, CT: Yale University Press, 2014), 238.
2. Eugene O'Neill, *Nine Plays by Eugene O'Neill* (New York: The Modern Library, 1952), 39.
3. Ibid., 44.
4. Ibid.
5. Ibid., 58.
6. Ibid., 65.
7. Ibid., 82.
8. Ibid., 85.
9. Ibid., 88.
10. Arthur Gelb and Barbara Gelb, *O'Neill* (New York: Random House, 1964), 499.
11. Dowling, 245.
12. Jordan Y. Miller, *Eugene O'Neill and the American Critic* (Hamden, CT: Archon Books, 1962), 356–358.
13. Ibid., 358.
14. *Nine Plays*, 107.
15. Ibid., 126.
16. Miller, 274–276.
17. Michael Manheim, ed., *The Cambridge Companion to Eugene O'Neill* (New York: Cambridge University Press, 1998), 153.
18. Jordan Y. Miller, *American Drama Between the Wars: A Critical History* (Boston: Twayne Publishers, 1991), 67.
19. Doris Alexander, *Eugene O'Neill's Creative Struggle: The Decisive Decade, 1924–1933* (University Park, PA: Pennsylvania State University Press, 1992), 30.
20. *Nine Plays*, 156.
21. Ibid., 161.

22. Ibid., 172.

23. Ibid., 192.

24. Ibid., 201.

25. Ibid.

26. Ibid., 165.

27. Ibid., 174.

28. Ibid., 198.

29. Ibid., 205.

30. Margaret L. Randald, *Cambridge Companion to Eugene O'Neill*, 65.

Chapter 5. O'Neill Examines the Human Psyche vs. Modern Values

1. Eugene O'Neill, Letter to Richard Dana Skinner, February 1934, Box 8, EON Mss. Quoted in John Patrick Diggins, *Eugene O'Neill's America*, 186.

2. Ibid., 30)

3. Louis Sheaffer, *O'Neill: Son and Artist* (Boston: Little, Brown & Co., 1973), 171–172.

4. Ibid., 310.

5. Ibid., 315.

6. Eugene O'Neill, *Nine Plays by Eugene O'Neill* (New York: The Modern Library, 1952), 331.

7. Ibid., 333.

8. Ibid., 337.

9. Ibid., 347.

10. Ibid., 361.

11. Ibid., 368.

12. Ibid., 374.

13. Arthur Gelb and Barbara Gelb, *O'Neill* (New York: Random House, 1964), 593.

14. Jordan Y. Miller, *Eugene O'Neill and the American Critic* (Hamden, CT: Archon Books, 1962), 393.

15. Ibid., 395.

16. *Nine Plays*, 397.

17. Ibid., 479.

18. Travis Bogard and Jackson R. Bryer, eds., *Selected Letters of Eugene O'Neill* (New Haven, CT: Yale University Press, 1988), 226.

19. Robert M. Dowling, *Eugene O'Neill: A Life in Four Acts* (New Haven, CT: Yale University Press, 2014), 264.

20. Bogard and Bryer, 233.

21. Ibid., 235.

22. Ibid., 239.

23. Doris Alexander, *Eugene O'Neill's Creative Struggle: The Decisive Decade, 1924–1933* (University Park, PA: Pennsylvania State University Press, 1992), 111.

24. *Nine Plays*, 630.

25. Ibid., 520.

26. Ibid., 669.

27. Ibid., 603.

28. Ibid., 667.

29. Ibid., 668.

30. Ibid., 674.

31. Ibid., 681.

32. Bogard and Bryer, 270.

33. Miller, 427–428.

34. Ibid., 427.

35. Ibid., 428.

36. Eugene O'Neill, *Eugene O'Neill: Complete Plays, 1932–1943* (New York: Library of America, 1988), 3:980.

Chapter 6. O'Neill Brings Modernism to Studies of Good and Evil

1. Mark W. Estrin, ed., *Conversations with Eugene O'Neill* (Jackson, MS: University Press of Mississippi, 1990), 107.

2. Carlotta O'Neill, quoted in Robert M. Dowling, *Eugene O'Neill: A Life in Four Acts* (New Haven, CT: Yale University Press, 2014), 367.

3. Eugene O'Neill, *The Plays of Eugene O'Neill* (New York: Random House, 1964), 3:473.

4. Ibid., 454.

5. Ibid., 482.

6. Louis Sheaffer, *O'Neill: Son and Artist* (Boston: Little, Brown & Co., 1973), 324.

7. Travis Bogard and Jackson R. Bryer, eds., *Selected Letters of Eugene O'Neill* (New Haven, CT: Yale University Press, 1988), 368.

8. Eugene O'Neill, *Nine Plays by Eugene O'Neill* (New York: Modern Library, 1952), 699.

9. Ibid., 716.

10. Ibid., 696.

11. Ibid., 722.

12. Ibid., 709.

13. Ibid., 737.

14. Ibid., 738.

15. Ibid., 740.

16. Ibid., 761.

17. Ibid., 748.

18. Ibid., 759.

19. Ibid., 802.

20. Ibid., 856.

21. Ibid., 867.

22. Jackson Bryer and Robert Dowling, eds., *Eugene O'Neill: The Contemporary Reviews* (New York: Cambridge University Press, 2014), 694.

23. *The Plays of Eugene O'Neill*, 3:493–494.

24. Ibid., 518.

25. Ibid., 549.

26. Ibid., 542.

27. Ibid.

28. Brooks Atkinson, *The Contemporary Reviews*, 763

29. Bernard Sobel, *The Contemporary Reviews*, 774.

Chapter 7. "Those Dear Old Days!": O'Neill Takes a Look From the Past

1. Stephen A. Black, *Eugene O'Neill: Beyond Mourning and Tragedy* (New Haven, CT: Yale University Press, 1999), 390.

2. Travis Bogard, *Contour in Time: The Plays of Eugene O'Neill* (New York: Oxford University Press, 1988), 355.

3. Eugene O'Neill, *The Plays of Eugene O'Neill* (New York: Random House, 1964), 3:571.

4. Travis Bogard and Jackson R. Bryer, eds., *Selected Letters of Eugene O'Neill* (New Haven, CT: Yale University Press, 1988), 501.

5. Bogard, *Contour in Time*, 356.

6. Eugene O'Neill, *Eugene O'Neill: Complete Plays, 1932–1943* (New York: Library of America, 1988), 3:11.

7. Ibid., 84.

8. Ibid.

9. Ibid., 87.

10. Bogard and Bryer, *Selected Letters*, 486.

11. "Nobel Prize for Literature," National Park Service, accessed January 1, 2016, www.nps.gov/euon/nobel-prize-for-literature.htm.

12. Bogard and Bryer, *Selected Letters*, 501.

13. Ibid.

14. Ibid., 502.

15. *Eugene O'Neill: Complete Plays, 1932–1943*, 570.

16. Ibid., 571.

17. Ibid., 575.

18. Ibid., 592.

19. Ibid., 629.
20. Ibid., 703.
21. John Patrick Diggins, *Eugene O'Neill's America* (Chicago: University of Chicago Press, 2007), 241.
22. Ibid., 210.
23. *The Plays of Eugene O'Neill*, 3:81.
24. *Eugene O'Neill: Complete Plays, 1932–1943*, 214.
25. Jordan Y. Miller, *Eugene O'Neill and the American Critic* (Hamden, CT: Archon Books, 1962), 89.
26. *Eugene O'Neill: Complete Plays, 1932–1943*, 273.
27. Ibid.
28. George Freedly in Jackson Bryer and Robert Dowling, eds., *Eugene O'Neill: The Contemporary Reviews* (New York: Cambridge University Press, 2014), 809.

Chapter 8. "May You Rest Forever in Forgiveness and Peace". O'Neill Banishes His Ghosts

1. Travis Bogard and Jackson R. Bryer, eds., *Selected Letters of Eugene O'Neill* (New Haven, CT: Yale University Press, 1988), 566.
2. Eugene O'Neill, Preface, *A Moon for the Misbegotten* (New York: Random House, 1952).
3. Travis Bogard, *Contour in Time: The Plays of Eugene O'Neill* (New York: Oxford University Press, 1988), 428.
4. Nancy L. Roberts and Arthur W. Roberts, eds., *"As Ever, Gene": The Letters of Eugene O'Neill to George Jean Nathan* (Cranbury, NJ: Fairleigh Dickinson University Press/ Associated University Presses, 1987), 202.
5. Eugene O'Neill, *Eugene O'Neill: Complete Plays, 1932–1943* (New York: Library of America, 1988), 3:714.
6. Ibid., 828.
7. Ibid., 819.
8. Ibid., 758.

9. John Patrick Diggins, *Eugene O'Neill's America* (Chicago: University of Chicago Press, 2007), 185.

10. *Eugene O'Neill: Complete Plays, 1932–1943*, 759.

11. Laurin Porter, *The Banished Prince: Time, Memory, and Ritual in the Late Plays of Eugene O'Neill* (Ann Arbor, MI: UMI Research Press, 1988), 89.

12. Ibid.

13. Jordan Y. Miller, *Eugene O'Neill and the American Critic* (Hamden, CT: Archon Books, 1962), 385–387.

14. Ibid., 387.

15. Ibid., 384–385.

16. O'Neill, *A Moon for the Misbegotten*, 8.

17. Ibid., 92.

18. Ibid., 37.

19. Ibid., 35.

20. Ibid., 37.

21. Ibid., 102–103.

22. Ibid.

23. Ibid., 135.

24. *Eugene O'Neill: Complete Plays, 1932–1943*, 923.

25. Ibid., 140.

26. Ibid., 147.

27. Ibid., 174.

28. Ibid., 177.

29. Bogard, *Contour in Time*, 457.

30. Ibid., 458.

31. Miller, 401–402.

32. Elyse Sommer, "A Moon for the Misbegotten," *CurtainUp*, 2008, curtainup.com/moon for the misbegotten.html.

Chapter 9. "The Father of Us All": O'Neill Lives Into the 21st Century

1. Alexis Solosky, "Brian Dennehy: 'My Director Says I Have More Rage Than Anyone He's Known,'" *The Guardian*, February 12, 2015, www.theguardian.com/stage/2015/feb/12/brian-dennehy-eugene-oneill-iceman-cometh-brooklyn-academy-music.

2. Louis Schaeffer, *O'Neill: Son and Artist* (Boston: Little Brown & Co., 1973), 408.

3. Leonard Maltin, *Leonard Maltin's Classic Movie Guide* (New York: Plume/Penguin Group, 2005), 18.

4. Philip Kolin, "The Early Plays of Tennessee Williams," Scholars Panel, The Tennessee Williams Annual Review, 2005, www.tennesseewilliamsstudies.org/journal/work.php?ID=63.

5. Tennessee Williams, 1956 interview, in Arthur Gelb and Barbara Gelb, *O'Neill: Life With Monte Cristo* (New York: Applause Books, 2002), 640.

6. Dotson Rader, *Tennessee: Cry of the Heart* (New York: Doubleday and Company, 1985), 285.

7. Dominic Cavendish, "Eugene O'Neill's rare Sea Plays sail back on to the stage," *The Telegraph*, January 20, 2012, www.telegraph.co.uk/culture/theatre/theatre-features/9027463/Eugene-ONeills-rare-Sea-Plays-sail-back-on-to-the-stage.html.

8. Susannah Clapp, "The Hairy Ape review—Carvel is a man of steel," *The Guardian*, November 1, 2015, www.theguardian.com/stage/2015/nov/01/hairy-ape-eugene-oneill-bertie-carvel-observer-review.

9. Matt Wolf, "Review: Mourning Becomes Electra," *Variety*, December 2, 2003, variety.com/2003/legit/reviews/mourning-becomes-electra-5-1200537673/.

10. Martin Denton, "A Moon for the Misbegotten 2006–07," *NYTheatre*, April 13, 2007, www.nytheatre.com/Review/martin-denton-2007-4-13-a-moon-for-the-misbegotten.

11. Michael Billington, "Long Day's Journey Into Night—review," *The Guardian*, April 10, 2012, http://www.theguardian.com/stage/2012/apr/10/long-day-journey-night-review.

12. Alexis Solosky, "Brian Dennehy: 'My Director Says I Have More Rage Than Anyone He's Known,'" *The Guardian*, February 12, 2015, www.theguardian.com/stage/2015/feb/12/brian-dennehy-eugene-oneill-iceman-cometh-brooklyn-academy-music.

13. Jeffrey Sweet, *The O'Neill: The Transformation of Modern American Theater* (New Haven, CT: Yale University Press, 2014) p, ix.

14. Ibid.

15. Ibid., xii.

16. Ibid.

17. Carlotta Monterey O'Neill to George C. White, August 3, 1964, O'Neill Theater Center, July 6, 2007, www.oneilltheatercenter.org/about/history.htm.

18. Sweet, 187.

19. "The 'Ah, Wilderness!' Years 1888–1914," booklet published by the Eugene O'Neill Theatre Center, 1996.

20. Sweet, 289.

21. Ibid., 290.

22. John Patrick Diggins, *Eugene O'Neill's America* (Chicago: University of Chicago Press, 2007), 1.

23. Eugene O'Neill to Mary Ann Clark, August 8, 1923, in Stephen A. Black, *Eugene O'Neill: Beyond Mourning and Tragedy* (New Haven, CT: Yale University Press, 1999), vii.

LITERARY TERMS

expressionism—A style of artistic presentation that flourished in European theatre from about 1910 through the 1920s. It was a response to the Industrial Revolution and showed humans had become lost, machine-like creatures. Expressionism challenged capitalism and materialist values, and used distorted imagery to portray the human condition. O'Neill used elements of expressionism in *The Hairy Ape, The Great God Brown,* and *Dynamo.*

melodrama—This style of playwriting involved a serious plot that was initiated and kept in motion by the designs of a villain or villains. Good and evil were white and black, sharply differentiated. Characters were mainly two-dimensional. Moral issues were simplistic. The villain's power was destroyed at the end; the good achieved happiness and a reward. Virtue always triumphed. Since "real life" is seldom played out in this manner, melodrama is the opposite of realism. Playwrights like O'Neill, raised on the nineteenth-century melodrama *The Count of Monte Cristo,* preferred naturalism and selective realism.

modernism—This term refers to the belief that a play need not be staged in exactly the same style, language, and dialect as originally written by the author. A modernist director selects from many new styles and resolutions, but the basic message of the author must be respected and clearly revealed.

naturalism   In art or literature, the philosophy of portraying life as it naturally is, without idealization.

point of view—In playwriting, the author chooses what will be the prominent viewpoint of the work. It can belong to the hidden author or one main character who acts as a major spokesperson or even the narrator of the story. Point of view for O'Neill differed depending on the needs of each play.

realism—An approach in playwriting to present characters and situations as they would appear in real life. Using direct observation, realistic writers present society objectively.

repertory theatre—In the beginning, this was a theatre that did several different plays in a given week. It also came to mean in both England and America a regional theatre that was nonprofit, produced limited runs of plays, and was devoted more to quality artistic work than commercial success. Now, in America, most larger cities have a repertory theatre. They do both revivals and new works, and some share producing costs and send productions from city to city.

satire—Satirical playwrights write a dark style of comedy that not only makes us laugh but also reveals the hypocrisy and pretentiousness of our society. Satire is more intellectual and character-oriented than farce is.

socialism—This political and economic movement began in the eighteenth century. Socialism requires the state or community to give equal care and protection to all citizens, regardless of how much they contribute financially. Many artists during O'Neill's youth promoted socialism. They tried to show the positive side of this movement in their work.

style—In theatre, style comes from a mode of expression and method of presentation. Dramatists' style is based on what they perceive is truth and reality. Style also results from how a dramatist uses his characters, language, visual sets and action. Also, style can come from how the play itself is produced in a theatre. Different "styles" of production can be applied to the same script.

symbol—Something that stands for, represents or suggests another thing.

symbolism—The representation of things by use of symbols.

Theatre Guild—Because a syndicate owned most of the New York playhouses, new dramatists were often locked out. Only commercially viable plays were produced. The Theatre Guild of New York was organized in 1919 to introduce new authors and produce radical works by Europeans and Americans. It continued to grow as a producing company that helped O'Neill's career and supported the work of Robert Sherwood, Maxwell Anderson, Sidney Howard, William Saroyan, William Inge, and Philip Barry.

tragedy—A form of serious drama involving persons caught in calamitous circumstances. The audience grows fearful and apprehensive for characters who suffer, and admires their courage. Tragedy was the earliest form of western drama, created by classical Greek authors. Tragedy explores the great issues of human cruelty, fate that doles out injustice, the limits of human endurance, and the triumph of the spirit. O'Neill wrote tragedy primarily using eighteenth- through twentieth-century American characters and society.

Major Works by Eugene O'Neill

NOTE: Dates correspond to the years the plays were first produced.

Beyond the Horizon (1920)
The Emperor Jones (1920)
Anna Christie (1921)
The Hairy Ape (1922)
All God's Chillun Got Wings (1924)
Desire Under the Elms (1924)
The Fountain (1925)
The Great God Brown (1926)
Lazarus Laughed (1928)
Marco Millions (1928)
Strange Interlude (1928)
Dynamo (1929)
Mourning Becomes Electra (1931)
Ah, Wilderness! (1933)
Days Without End (1934)
The Iceman Cometh (1946)
A Moon for the Misbegotten (1947)
Long Day's Journey Into Night (1956)
A Touch of the Poet (1957)

FURTHER READING

Bryer, Jackson, and Robert M. Dowling, eds. *Eugene O'Neill: The Contemporary Reviews*. New York: Cambridge University Press, 2014.

Diggins, John Patrick. *Eugene O'Neill's America*. Chicago: University of Chicago Press, 2007.

Dowling, Robert. *Eugene O'Neill: A Life in Four Acts*. New Haven: Yale University Press, 2014.

Gelb, Arthur, and Barbara Gelb. *O'Neill: Life with Monte Cristo*. New York: Applause Books, 2000.

Sheaffer, Louis. *O'Neill: Son and Playwright*. New York: Cooper Square Press, 2002.

Sweet, Jeffrey. *The O'Neill: The Transformation of Modern American Theater*. New Haven, CT: Yale University Press, 2014.

WEBSITES

Electronic Eugene O'Neill Archive
www.eoneill.com
An electronic archive and forum devoted to Eugene O'Neill Theater Center and all its programs, awards, and activities.

Eugene O'Neill Foundation, Tao House
www.eugeneoneill.org
News and events related to O'Neill as well as a searchable online collection of works.

Eugene O'Neill Society
www.eugeneoneillsociety.org.
Promotes an appreciation for the playwright through publications, performances, and education.

Eugene O'Neill: A Documentary Film
www.pbs.org/wgbh/amex/oneill
Site for Ric Burns's documentary.

Eugene O'Neill: A Glory of Ghosts
www.pbs.org/wnet/americanmasters/database/oneill_e.html
Site for the O'Neill documentary film by Perry Miller Adato.

Eugene O'Neill Theatre Center Facebook Page
www.facebook.com/oneilltheatercenter/?fref=ts
Features news, activities, awards, photos, and performances by the staff and participants at the EOTC.

INDEX